John Muir's
# "Stickeen"
## *and the*
# Lessons
# *of* Nature

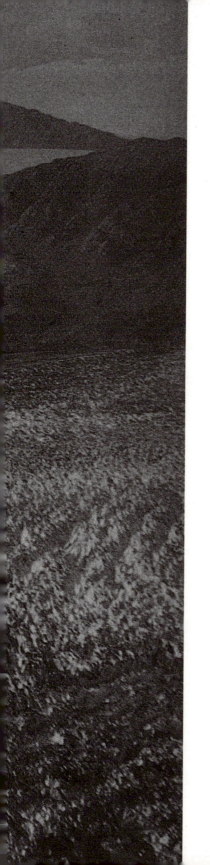

# John Muir's
# "Stickeen"
## and the
# Lessons
## of Nature

## Ronald H. Limbaugh

**University of Alaska Press**
**Fairbanks, Alaska**

Library of Congress Cataloging-in-Publication Data

Limbaugh, Ronald H.
    John Muir's "Stickeen" and the lessons of nature / Ronald H.
Limbaugh.
        p.    cm.
    Includes bibliographical references (p.      ) and index.
    ISBN 0-912006-84-6 (cloth : alk. paper)
    1. Muir, John, 1838–1914. Stickeen. 2. Dogs--Alaska--Anecdotes.
3. Muir, John, 1838–1914. I. Muir, John, 1838–1914. Stickeen.
II. Title.
SF426.2.L56  1996                                            96-5172
813'.4--dc20                                                      CIP

The copyrighted words of John Muir including "Journal of 1880 from
Wrangel Up Coast To Sum Dum Takou," are printed by permission.
Copyright 1984, by the Muir-Hanna Trust.

Printed in the United States by Thomson-Shore, Inc.

This publication was printed on acid-free paper that meets the minimum
requirements of American National Standard for Information Sciences-
Permanence for Paper for Printed Library Materials, ANSI Z39.48-1984.

Publication coordination by Deborah Van Stone.
Publication design and production by Paula Elmes.
Text face is Sabon; display face is RunicMT.

Dustjacket photograph: Muir at his desk in the "scribble den" at Martinez,
about 1892. Holt-Atherton Library, University of the Pacific.

Endpage photograph: The front of Muir Glacier, ca.1890. The photographer
is unknown. John Muir Papers, in Holt-Atherton Library, University of the
Pacific. (Microform edition, Fiche 10/0486)

*Dedicated to Richard Hanna and Walter Muir*
*Who carefully preserved and generously donated their*
*grandfather's books so that others might learn from them.*

—RONALD H. LIMBAUGH

# Contents

# Illustrations

# Preface

More than a century has passed since John Muir and a dog named Stickeen walked on a treacherous glacier in Alaska. The narrative of their journey together was first published as a magazine article in 1897 and has been reprinted many times since.[1] Contemporary reviewers were enthralled. Muir's editor, Robert Underwood Johnson, said it was "one of the finest studies of dogliness in all literature."[2] After the book version came out in 1909, a testy Oregon reviewer said the story "makes cheap and impossible such dog-books as Jack London and others of that ilk inflict on long-suffering typewriters."[3] California poet Edwin Markham said Muir's tale takes its place beside "The Dog of Flanders" and "Rab" as one of the all-time great dog stories.[4] Muir's touchy friend John Burroughs, more reserved than Markham but with better credentials as a critic of nature writing, said it was "almost equal to 'Rab and his friends,'" John Brown's Victorian story of a Scottish Mastiff.[5] Much later, wilderness defender Howard Zahniser, writing in 1938 on the centennial of Muir's birth, praised "Stickeen" as simply the "best story of a dog that I have ever read."[6]

Time has mellowed our perspective on Muir and his work. "Stickeen" still finds a ready market among wilderness friends and Muir fanciers, but it occupies no literary pedestal. The published version deals only superficially with a fundamental part of the American experience, the relationship between humans and nature. It only hints at the meaning of that relationship and ends without exploring what nature is and how we interact with it. As Millard Davis once observed, Muir had superlative descriptive skills but "seems not able to get beyond the thought of reproducing the scene."[7]

In a recent critical appraisal of Muir's writings, Peter Fritzell demonstrates that Muir's most popular works did not challenge conventional American attitudes toward nature. His writing, unlike Thoreau's, "tends to become a combination of geobiotic science and what is sometimes called nature appreciation." Muir's popularity as a nature writer rested upon the public perception that his descriptive talents satisfied their yen for the exotic and exciting but did not run counter to their fundamental beliefs.[8]

While Fritzell did not cite "Stickeen" among those Muir writings he inspected, the criticism is well taken so far as it goes. The dog story might well have been included in his sampler of Muir's nature writing, for the published versions conform basically to the descriptive attributes Fritzell found in *Mountains of California, My First Summer in the Sierra,* and other popular Muir texts cited in his bibliography.[9] But often overlooked in assessing Muir's literary impact is the discrepancy between his published and unpublished writings. In matters of conservation and preservation the discrepancy is small, for Muir's *raison d'être* after 1890 was to save Yosemite and Hetch Hetchy and the other great wild landscapes he knew intimately. The private Muir and the public Muir during those epic struggles were almost one and the same. But on other matters of public concern Muir was more discreet, expressing views in private that he did not express openly. In most cases this censorship was self-imposed, for Muir was reluctant to upset his family or his popularity with publishers. Yet almost exactly a century ago, Muir found an opportunity to address basic questions about animals and their role in nature in a story that educated as well as entertained. In "Stickeen" he started to take a risk he never took before in writing about animals, but his editor intervened and Muir acquiesced. The published versions left out many of the lessons he initially wanted to teach.[10]

John Muir told his friends "Stickeen" was the hardest story he had ever composed. Reading the published version nearly eighty years later, I could not understand why at first. After all, from a writer's perspective the story line is uncomplicated. Drafting a first-person descriptive narrative of an exciting single event was one of my first assignments as a college freshman. Now, after nearly twenty years of working with the Muir papers, reading all the preliminary manuscripts and relevant correspondence, tracing the origins of key words, ideas, and phrases, and following the convoluted literary spoor left behind in the marginalia and endnotes of more than one hundred books from his personal library, I have begun to understand what Muir meant.[11]

Although its popularity has remained high for nearly a century, "Stickeen" has never ranked among Muir's most important writings. Muir himself originally considered it a mere anecdote, told to friends as an after-dinner story over cigars and good wine. Why, then, should any scholar spend the time tracing its origins and development, when the standard pattern of literary criticism is to ignore the "minor" pieces in an author's career as relatively unimportant to understanding the essence of a writer? I argue that in Muir's case the original version of "Stickeen" was much more than a minor piece. It began as an anecdote but grew in importance over a seventeen-year period.

With the possible exception of *Travels in Alaska*, no better example can be found than "Stickeen" to illustrate Muir's laborious writing process. From all the "Stickeen" sources that have been identified, including holographic journals, correspondence, notes, draft pages, and revisions, one can reconstruct the step-by-step, multilayered method he used to build a manuscript from first-hand observation to finished product. "Stickeen" is also quite different in style and substance from *Travels* and other nature writings by Muir. Most of his best-known works are travelogues like *A Thousand-Mile Walk to the Gulf* and *My First Summer in the Sierra*, polished descriptive narratives such as *The Mountains of California* and *Our National Parks,* or reminiscences like *The Story of My Boyhood and Youth*. The dog story, in contrast, is an adventure story whose significance has heretofore not been recognized by scholars. The version Muir wanted to publish is a singular example of his literary creativity and how it was influenced by the swirl of events and ideas at the turn of the nineteenth century. Moreover, it is the only literary product from Muir's pen that can be directly and extensively linked to ideas formulated from the books of his personal library. Indeed, it is the only work he composed literally on the back pages of his private book collection. Studying its origin and evolution is essential to understanding Muir's development as a writer and as an advocate for the moral equality of all species.

This study could never have been undertaken without the encouragement and support of my colleagues at the University of the Pacific. I am particularly grateful for the sabbatical leaves accorded me in the spring of 1988 and in the spring of 1993. The Rockwell Hunt Chair of California History, which I have held since 1989, has also provided substantial assistance in funding the costs of travel to research libraries and archives during the last four years.

My work has been immensely aided by the cooperation of members of the Muir-Hanna families. Unfortunately, death has recently claimed two family members who helped make this project possible: Mrs. Sherry Hanna, the *de facto* family archivist and caretaker of the family cemetery in Martinez, and Richard Hanna, who gave to the Holt-Atherton Library both his 800-volume collection of his grandfather's books and the bookcases Muir used to store them in the "big house" in Martinez, now known as the

Muir-Strentzel Home. Walter Muir, only surviving son of Muir's younger daughter Helen, provided important clues to the division of Muir's library at the time of his death in 1914, and to the subsequent donation of Helen's share of the books to the Huntington Library. The late Mrs. Margaret Swett Plummer also graciously supplied information and resources on the Muir-Swett relationship.

For their generous assistance in providing access to the Muir books and papers, I am grateful to Ms. Daryl Morrison and the staff at the Holt-Atherton Library at the University of the Pacific, and to Alan Jutzi and the staff at the Huntington Library. I also wish to acknowledge the help of librarians at the California State Library in Sacramento, the Shields Library of the University of California at Davis, the Bancroft Library at the University of California at Berkeley, the Beinecke Library at Yale, and the Houghton Library at Harvard.

All of these important library collections deserve public recognition and support.

I am particularly indebted to the following individuals who critically reviewed the manuscript in whole or in part: Frank Buske, Tucson, Arizona; Michael Cohen, Southern Utah State College; James D. Heffernan and Sally M. Miller, University of the Pacific; Richard J. Orsi, Hayward State University; and the late Irving Stone, Beverly Hills, California.

I hope this publication will stimulate other scholars to explore the remarkable mind of Muir through the rich documentary collection he left behind.

# Endnotes

1. Most recently a version of the story appeared in *Muir Among the Animals: The Wildlife Writings of John Muir*, ed. by Lisa Mighetto (San Francisco: Sierra Club Books, c1986), 83–94.

2.  Robert U. Johnson, *Remembered Yesterdays* (Boston: Little, Brown, 1923), 284.

3.  Undated clipping from [Portland] *Sunday Oregonian,* in Series VI: Stickeen Reviews, John Muir Papers, Holt-Atherton Library, University of the Pacific, hereafter JMP UOPWA.

4.  Review in *San Francisco Examiner,* September 11, 1909, in Series VI: Stickeen Reviews, JMP UOPWA.

5.  John Burroughs, *The Life and Letters of John Burroughs,* ed. by Clara Barrus, v. 1 (Boston & NY: Houghton Mifflin, 1925), 360.

6.  "The Story of a Dog—and John Muir," *National Nature News* 2 (March 28, 1938): 1, 7, in Series VI: Stickeen Reviews, JMP UOPWA.

7.  Millard C. Davis, "The Influence of Emerson, Thoreau and Whitman on the Early American Naturalists John Muir and John Burroughs," *Living Wilderness* (Winter, 1966), 21.

8.  Peter A. Fritzell, *Nature Writing and America: Essays Upon a Cultural Type* (Ames: Iowa State Univ. Press, c1990), 3–35; 75–76.

9.  Significantly, Fritzell did not mention *A Thousand-Mile Walk to the Gulf,* the book most often referred to by modern biographers and environmental activists in assessing Muir's place in the history of environmental activism.

10. Judson D. McGehee noted this reticence in a 1958 dissertation but did not venture an explanation. He also criticized Muir's published writings for their "limited range" of ideas and lack of philosophical depth. Judson D. McGehee, "The Nature Essay as a Literary Genre: an Intrinsic Study of the Works of Six English and American Nature Writers" (Ph.D dissertation, University of Michigan, 1958), 30.

11. Muir's 1897 draft was published as "An Adventure with a Dog and a Glacier," *The Century Magazine* 54 (September 1897): 769–775. The book was published as *Stickeen* (Boston & New York: Houghton Mifflin, 1909). In the 1980s Muir's correspondence, manuscripts, journals, and notes were published in *The John Muir Papers, 1858–1957.* Microform Edition. Ronald H. Limbaugh and Kirsten Lewis, eds. (Alexandria, Va: Chadwyck-Healey, Inc., 1986), 51 reels & 53 fiche. See also *The Guide and Index to the Microform Edition of the John Muir Papers* (Chadwyck-Healey, Inc., 1986). Hereinafter all references to the Microform Edition will be cited by the location code JMP UOPWA, followed by reel and frame numbers for the item.

# John Muir's

# "Stickeen"

## and the

# Lessons of Nature

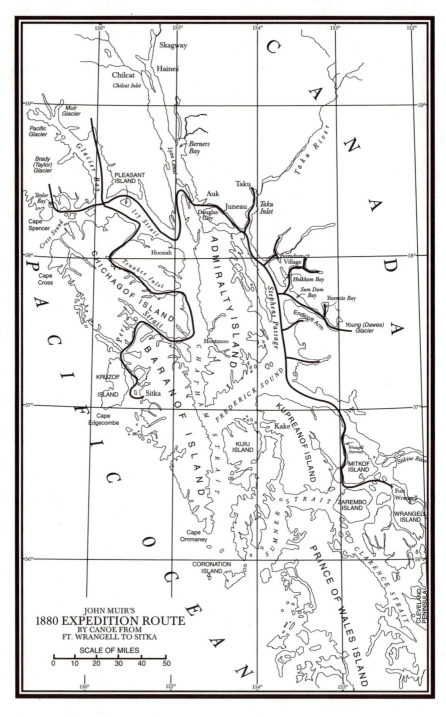

*Redrawn from S. Hall Young,* Alaska Days with John Muir *(New York: Fleming H. Revell Co., 1915.*

# One

# Muir and Stickeen on the Taylor Glacier

There's more than instinct in the jocund play
Of 'Jack', the little Scot, dear as a child
Alas! that arrogance has so misstyled
The intelligence of brutes, and said them nay
At this life's close. Denying them, there may
Be no Supreme law such as man has filed
Against them. I could well be reconciled
To share with all of them a judgment-day
And life eternal. Not a blasphemous thought
(Witness, O Thou who knowest me) is mine:
But then dog's life, so innocent, is fraught
With intimation of such high design
That I could wish we never had been taught
To think man only holds the spark divine.[1]

John Muir had an abiding interest in dogs. He never tired of reading about them, and occasionally he wrote about them. In his books and articles they invariably appear with complex, nearly human personalities, each worth special consideration and respect.[2] The poem by John Boner quoted above

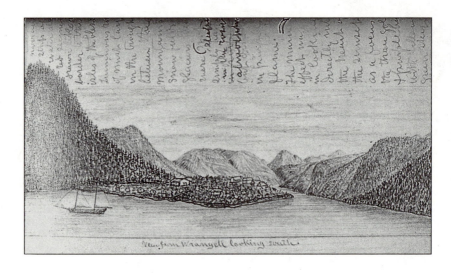

*Ft. Wrangell as Muir sketched it in 1879.*

reflected Muir's own thoughts. About 1900 it appeared in a newspaper Muir read, and he clipped it for his files. Perhaps it was inspired by Muir's own dog story, published in *Century* in 1897.

The story of "Stickeen" long lay in John Muir's memory before it was recorded in print. Like a work of art, it was not reality but a version of reality, an interpretation of a single day's adventure rather than simple description. The setting was an Alaskan glacier in the summer of 1880. Muir was then forty-two, an experienced naturalist and accomplished author whose scientific treatises and popular articles were already beginning to attract national attention.

Americans knew almost nothing of Alaska before 1867, when it was acquired by the United States, and very little from 1867 until the Klondike gold rush in the late 1890s. Distance, public ignorance, congressional indifference, preoccupation with post-Civil War politics, and the icebox myth all played a role in discouraging American interest. Aside from a few regional gold

*Muir sketched this Indian canoe in 1879. It is similar to the one used on the 1880 trip.*

and fur hunters along the southern panhandle, exploring America's first non-contiguous territory was left to a few prospectors and to a handful of individual scientists, journalists, and naturalists.[3] Most Americans stayed away until the 1880s, when a modest tourist industry, largely confined to the economic elite, began to develop along the Alaskan Panhandle. Contributing significantly to the rise of that industry was John Muir, the best known and most widely read of the early explorers. His forty-one San Francisco *Bulletin* articles between 1879 and 1882 were widely reprinted across the United States.[4]

  Muir's interest in Alaska followed naturally from his Sierra glacial studies. In July 1879, traveling with a group of Presbyterian clergy,[5] he began the first of seven trips to the far North. He reached Wrangell via steamship through Alaska's Inside Passage and spent the next six months exploring the coastal waters and the icy fiords of the Alexander Archipelago. On one

*S. Hall Young, Muir's missionary companion. Photograph by W. H. Towne, ca. 1885.*

side trip he ventured up the Stikine River,[6] known to placer miners since the early 1860s, when a modest gold strike had occurred. More than a decade later another boom followed in the Cassiar region, but neither lasted very long.[7] Mining held no interest for Muir, who considered it at best a dubious enterprise. He had come for "ice work," and he found it in abundance in Glacier Bay, a spectacular "fountain" of icebergs he was the first to explore.[8]

In July 1880 he began his second trip North, intending to retrace his earlier route and examine more carefully the rivers of ice pouring into the Gulf of Alaska. This time credentialed as correspondent for the *Bulletin*, he left behind his bride of three months. At Fort Wrangell he rejoined the Reverend Samuel Hall Young, a Presbyterian missionary with a penchant for exploration who had accompanied him the year before. To assist them they recruited three local Indians, Hunter Joe, Smart Billy, and Captain Tyeen, the latter commanding the twenty-five-foot canoe used by the party. At the last minute they also took aboard Young's little mongrel dog, named after one of the villages Young served. Described by his owner as "the handsomest dog I have ever known,"[9] but by Muir as "a small black dumpling of dullness,"[10] Stickeen gradually attached himself to the wandering Scot, whose crusty exterior concealed a sentimental affection for dogs.

After two weeks of travel and exploration along the Alexander Archipelago while heading north toward Glacier Bay, the party reached Taylor Bay in the evening and camped near the snout of an unexplored glacier.[11] Early the next morning, while the others slept, Muir ate a bite of bread and set out to explore the massive expanse of ice that stretched more than twenty miles inland.

We have only Muir's word for what happened that day, and we shall see details of the story change over a fifteen-year period. But the dog remained central to the story both in its verbal and written form. In the most familiar version, as Muir left camp the dog tagged along despite Muir's warning words and the foul weather. Crossing the glacier diagonally by following flow lines and jumping crevasses, Muir and the dog reached the opposite shore, traced the path for several miles, then headed back near dusk on a different route. As darkness loomed they entered a heavily crevassed area. Some gaps could be jumped, others had to be crossed by straddling or gingerly stepping on icy connecting bridges which Muir smoothed with his ice axe for Stickeen's benefit, while still others required long looping detours. Soggy from the rain, without food since the breakfast bread, nearly exhausted from the long walk, and handicapped by the dimming twilight, Muir and the dog soon found themselves stranded on an island with the only escape a badly deteriorated spiny ice bridge. How they made it across is the thrilling climax of the story.

The story Muir ultimately wrote for publication was not a true-life adventure but a parable on the worth of animals and their importance to mankind. That fiction grew from fact is clear by comparing Muir's original narrative in his 1880 journal with the final draft he submitted to *Century* in 1897.

The 1880 narrative that follows is vintage Muir, the indefatigable explorer, whose descriptive powers complement his infectious enthusiasm for wilderness in its most chaotic form. Together they capture the depth of emotional experience Romantics called the sublime.[12] This wild setting Muir later considered an essential backdrop for understanding the soul of Stickeen. But looking into dog nature was far from his mind when he sat down to record his first impressions of the 1880 trip. What impressed him most was the overpowering energy of raw wilderness.[13] Muir's shorthand spelling has been filled out where necessary for clarity, with added letters in braces { }. Muir's own additions are in brackets [ ].

## *Journal of 1880 from Wrangel up Coast to Sum Dum Takou*[14]

Set off early before anyone else in the camp had stirred not waiting for breakfast but eating a piece of bread. The morning was cold & wet, heavy rain driven by a strong wind roaring like a blast over the icey levels & over the woods on the mtns & over the jagged rocks & spires & chasms of the gl & filling all the broad valley in even structureless gloomy gray. Yet how inspiring it all was. I first pushed up in the face of the wind to the bend of the snout where a patch of forest is being carried away by the resisting onthrust of the snout, here about 400 ft h{igh}. In front of it there is a mor{aine}

lake about half a m{ile} in length around the margin of wh
are a consid number of trees standing kneedeep & dead of
course. Also a result of the advance of the ice. Also noticed a
few stumps well out on the flat showing that the present bare
raw condition of the flat 1 1/2 {miles} wide in front of the ice
was not the condition of 50 or 100 yrs ago. Pushing up thro
the ragged edge of the woods on the left margin the storm
increased in volume & I took shelter under a tree to enjoy it
& wait. Here the gl descending over an abrupt rock falls in
grand cascades while a stream swollen by the rain was now a
torrent wind rain ice current & water torrent in one grand
symphony . . .

   When the storm began to abate I took off my heavy
rubber boots with wh I had traveled the gl streams on the
mud & gravel flat & laid them on a log—where I might find
them on my way back & put on a pair of mtn shoes firmly
tied—tightened my belt shouldered my axe for cutting steps
on the ice cliffs & thus ready for rough work pushed on
regardless as possible of the mere rain. Making my way up a
steep granite slope burnished on its projecting bosses by the
gl where it flowed at a higher level, & incumbered by
bowlders stranded here & there & by the ruins all ground &
bruised of the ragged forest edge that had been uprooted by
the gl during its period quite recent of advance. I traced the
side of the gl for 2 or 3 ms finding everywhere indubitable
evidence of its having encroached on the wood wh here run
back along its edge for 15 or 20 ms under the projecting edge
of the vast ice river. I saw down beneath it for 50 ft or 20
logs & branches being crushed into pulp some of it fine
enough for paper. After uprooting the trees they are carried
along like other moraine material & where the slope of the
bank is not too great they are at length left stranded among
bowlders & gravel in & on the lateral moraine but where the

slope is too steep for them to rest on they fall back beneath the edge of the moving ice & carried forward against outswelling bosses & rigidly ground like wheat between the upper & nether millstones.

After thus tracing the margin of the gl for 3 ms or thereabouts I climbed by means of steps cut with my axe on to the top of its broad back & far as the eye could reach the ice level stretched indefinately away in the gray rainy sky a prairie of ice. The wind was now moderate though rain continued to fall copiously wh I did not mind much but there was a tendency in the low drooping draggliedged clouds to mist that made me hesitate about attempting to cross to the opposite side of the gl no trace could be seen of the mtns on the other side although only 6 or 7 ms away & in case the sky grew darker as it seemed inclined to do I feared I might get out of sight of land & in case the ice was badly crevassed might find difficulty in getting back. Lingering awhile & sauntering about in sight of land I found this side remarkably good as regards . . . crevasses. Nearly all were so narrow I could step across them almost anywhere while the wider ones were easily avoided. So I finally concluded to try it resolved to turn should any untoward developments appear on the way while I took my bearings occasionally with a pocket compass to enable me more surely to find my way back. The structure lines of the gl itself were however my main guide.

I set out crossing diagonally so as to strike the opposite bank about 5 or 6 miles above the snout. All went well I came to a deeply furrowed section about 2 ms wide where I had to zigzag in long tedious tucks or make narrow doublings tracing the edges of longitudinal furrows & chasms many of wh were 50 ft wide until I could find a bridge, oftentimes making the direct distance ten times over. The walking was good of its kind however & by dint of patient doubling & axe work on dangerous places I gained the opposite bank in about 3 hours.

Occasionally the clouds lifted a little revealing a few bold rock mtns sunk to the throat in the broad waving bosom of the grand icy sea wh encompassed them on all sides sweeping on forever & forever as we count time wearing them away giving them the shape they are destined to take when in the fullness of time they shall be parts of a landscape not yet born never yet has seen the sun. Ere I came lost sight of the mtn on the side I had left & came in sight of the other so that steering was easy. I often halted a moment to gaze down into the bonnie pure blue of the crevasses & to drink at the wells sunk in the living crystal on wh the rills & streams outspread over the iceland prairie never ceasing to admire their intense purity & the sweet gurgling & ringing of the currents smoothly gliding & swirling in the living flawless ethereal crystal. The rumbling too of the moulins or mills when a stream poured out of sight in glassy walled pits round as if bored with auger & of unknown depth. How interesting too were the cascades over the blue cliffs where streams fell into crevasses or slid almost noiselessly down slopes so smooth & frictionless as scarce to make them visible, or falling swirling into potholes. The round or oval wells howe[ve]r were perhaps the most beautiful of all from one to ten ft wide & one to 20 or 30 deep the water 20 pure almost invisible My widest views did not probably cover 15 ms but the rain & mist made distances seem much greater they were. On reaching the land again I found a large portion of the current sweeping around the shoulder of a mtn in a beautiful & bold curve towards the sea as if going out that way as one of the outlets of this great merdiglace. After leaving the main trunk it breaks into a magnificent uproar of pinnacles & spires in descending a steep portion of its channel & in a few miles falls into a lake which it fills with bergs. The snout is about 3 ms wide I first took this lake to be an arm of the sea but going down to it found it fresh & by my aneroid about 50 ft above sea level probably only seperated by moraine dam. as the main icy berg was a moraine much of wh is still above the water at high tide.

I had not time to get around the shores of the lake as it was by this time 5 o'clock & I had to make haste to recross the gl before dark wh would come on about 8. I therefore pushed back up the declivity of this lake branch of the gl & shaping my course by compass & by the structure lines of the ice set off from land out into the grand crystal prairie. All was so silent & so concent{rat}ed owing to the mist that I could not help but feel a certain pleasure in the grandeur about me not unmixed [revised later to "mixed"] with a dim sense of danger, [added later: "as if coming events were casting shadow over me"] for I was soon out of sight of land & the evening dusk that on cldy days precedes the real night gloom came stealing on while the ice was here the ice was there the ice was all around & no sound save the rumbling mills & the rattle of stones at long intervals as they were melted off their pedestals & sent to seek a new rest["ing places" added later]. But even these gl sounds were awanting at times in crevassed portions where the water all vanished as soon as it fell from the sky or was melted from the gl only the terribly earnest low roar of the wind or of some waterfall heard in the far dist coming through the damp sky.

After two hrs of hard work had been done I came into a wide area of crevasses of apalling depth & width close together & wh could not be passed apparently either up or down. I traced them with firm nerve developed by the danger making wide jumps poising cautiously on dizzy edges & after cutting a firm foothold taking wide crevasses at a grand leap

*Muir's sketch of his base camp at Taylor Bay, August 29–30, 1880.*

at once frightful and inspiring. Many a mile I thus made
mostly up & down with but little real headway running
much of the time as the danger of passing the night on the gl
became more & more imminent. This I could no doubt do
though it would be hard in [account of coldness of the
weather] my hungry chilled rainsoaked condition. In thread-
ing the maze of this crevassed region I had frequently to cross
bridges that were only knife edges for 20 or 30 ft straddling
them & cutting off their edges as I progressed like boys riding
a rail fence. No land in sight & the mist came lower &
darker I could not see far enough up or down to know how
best to work out of my difficulty, & how hard I worked
while yet there was hope of reaching camp a hope wh so fast
growing more dim like the sky for I could not allow myself to
stop on such ground after dark I could then but jump & try
to keep warm until morning [added later: "find a piece of flat

ice between the crevasses & dance there all night to the music of the winds & waters."] Many times I was put to my mettle but with firm nerve all the more unflinching as the dangers thickened I worked out of that terrible ice labirynth, & reached ordinary ice over wh with my blood fairly up I ran without fatigue every muscle glorying in its strength I knew by the ice-line, that every step was now taking me nearer the shore & soon it came in sight, a headland 5 ms back from the snout covered with spruces looming faintly but surely through the mist not more than two miles away. The ice proved good to the very bank wh I reached just at dusk then with glad strong strides I traced the edge & got over the dangerous rocks where the cascades are while yet in faint light lingered. Then I was safe & then too came limp weariness such as no ordinary work ever produces however hard. Wearily I stumbled down through a mile of woods full of fallen logs & bushes & wide clasping roots of devils clubs for spice to every faint blundering tumble. How glad to get out upon the smooth mud slope only a mile of sore but sure dragging of my poor limbs & then camp food & above all rest as only a mtneer may ever enjoy in this world.

Mr Y. & the Inds had become alarmed & were firing guns to guide me also built a grand fire & were counting on being compelled to seek me in the morning. A care not often applied to me. This is thus far the largest by far of all the gls I have ever walked on some 20 ms or more. Yet I have not yet seen its distant fountains so low & dense the clds. I saw back about 15 ms, & still it seemed to stretch away indefinately & with but little ascent thus accounting for its waste without giving bergs to the sea. It however wastes in bergs in two cakes by its wide mouths. The fact of its advance of late yrs is recognized with alarm by the Inds who sacrificed two stags to make it retreat to its old bounds fearing that it would wholly destroy their salmon fishing by cutting off the spawning grounds.

In comparing the above with the final draft reprinted later,[15] the most striking difference is the total lack of any reference, directly or indirectly, in the 1880 journal to a dog. Did Stickeen really exist or was he a product of the author's fertile imagination? Surely the dog was real; his presence was confirmed not only by a mention of the dog in one of Muir's 1880 letters to the San Francisco *Bulletin*[16] but also by the testimony of others, in particular Muir's missionary companion, S. Hall Young, whose own book on Muir is filled with references to "Stickeen" from the 1880 trip and who cooperated with Muir in writing a reminiscence about the dog.[17]

Why, then, did Muir leave the dog out of his journal? The most plausible answer is that Muir didn't recognize the dog's importance until the early 1890s. In the intervening years he had become a gentleman farmer with a handsome income and a generous wife. Muir scholars tend to exaggerate the frustrations Muir experienced in the 1880s. Exchanging the wild Yosemite days for a prosperous life in Alhambra Valley was a willful act that brought with it security and fortune, things he had never known before. Now down from the mountains, he supplemented the book of nature with the literal book, the aggregate knowledge of human-kind bound in cloth and hard leather. His expanding book collection indicated his intellectual growth, both made possible by time and affluence, two precious gifts he received from his indulgent and willing new in-laws and partners, the Strentzels. They gave him the instruments of a new education, and he richly repaid them by mastering the practical science of horticulture even as he immersed himself in the literature of the western world. The fortune he earned as a fruit farmer paled in comparison to the wealth of knowledge he gleaned from his books. They broadened and deepened his perspective on nature and life. The man who wrote the dog story in the 1890s was more reflective and philosophical than the effervescent explorer of earlier years.

Before composing the story, Muir told it time and again to family and friends. For fifteen years the story survived only as anecdote, part of its author's verbal repertoire. But the repeated tellings also polished it and enhanced its potential as literature. The development of this oral phase in the life of "Stickeen" is the subject of the next chapter.

# Endnotes

1.  John H. Boner, "Jack," poem in unidentified newspaper clipping, ca. 1897, John Muir Papers, Series VI, alpha-file "Animals-Dogs," Holt-Atherton Library, University of the Pacific, hereafter cited as JMP UOPWA.

2.  See, for example, Muir's comments in "The Story of My Boyhood and Youth." vol. 1 of *The Writings of John Muir*, ed. by William F. Badé (Boston and New York: Houghton Mifflin Co., 1916), 64–68; *My First Summer in the Sierra*, v. 2 of *Writings*, 5–6; *Our National Parks*, v. 6 of *Writings*, 191–92; 198–99.

3.  Morgan B. Sherwood, *Exploration of Alaska, 1865–1900* (1965; reprint, Fairbanks: University of Alaska Press, 1992), 2–7, 36–73.

4.  Frank Buske, "The Wilderness, the Frontier and the Literature of Alaska to 1914: John Muir, Jack London and Rex Beach" (Ph.D. Dissertation, Univ. of California at Davis, 1976), 36, 97–98. The most recent republication is *Letters from Alaska*, edited by Robert Engberg and Bruce Merrell (Madison: Univ. of Wisconsin Press, 1993).

5.  The clerics were en route to their recently established mission at Fort Wrangell. Ted C. Hinkley, "Sheldon Jackson and Benjamin Harrison," in *Alaska and Its History*, ed. by Morgan B. Sherwood (Seattle and London: Univ. of Washington Press, c1967), 295.

6.  "Stickine" was the accepted spelling for the river and the Indian people in southeast Alaska, and was in common use both before and after the 1880s. The variant spelling Muir most often used for the dog, probably because of its phonetic advantages. But he was inconsistent, especially in 1897 while he gathered data on the Stikine River and the Indians. S. Hall Young's reminiscence of 1897 spells the dog's name "Stickine", and occasionally Muir did the same. His story-title of "Stickeen," however, fixed the accepted spelling, even though in the same draft he used the variant at times—which the *Century* editors caught before publishing. The "Stickeen" spelling was not unique to Muir, however. His changing usage may have been influenced by Frederick Schwatka, the head of a polar expedition in which the brother of his *Century* editor participated. Schwatka's 1893 Alaska travel narrative used the phonetic spelling. Frederick Schwatka, *A Summer in Alaska* (St. Louis, MO: J. W. Henry, 1893), 27–28.

7.  Lewis Green, *The Boundary Hunters: Surveying the 141st Meridian and the Alaska Panhandle* (Vancouver & London: Univ. of British Columbia Press, c1982), 5–6, 47.

8.  Buske, "The Wilderness, the Frontier & the Literature of Alaska," xii, 36.
    Muir was the first to enter and explore the bay, but two years earlier a U.S. Army officer on a private trip "caught a glimpse" of it from Mt. Fairweather. Morgan B. Sherwood, *Exploration of Alaska, 1865–1900* (New Haven & London: Yale Univ. Press, 1965), 75–76. In 1980 Glacier Bay became a National Park & Preserve, with over 2.7 million acres in the wilderness area adjacent to the bay itself. U.S. National Park Service, *The National Parks: Index 1987* (Washington: Dept. of the Interior, 1987).

9.  S. Hall Young, *Alaska Days with John Muir* (New York: Fleming H. Revell, c1915), 130.

10. Muir holograph note on the endpages of John Brown, *Horae Subsecivae* (Edinburgh: David Douglas, 1889), vol. 1, in John Muir's personal library, in Holt-Atherton Library, University of the Pacific, hereafter cited as JML UOPWA.

11. Frank E. Buske, "Go to Alaska: Go and see," *Alaska Journal 9* (Summer 1979): 32.

12. Edward H. Foster, *The Civilized Wilderness: Backgrounds to American Romantic Literature, 1817–1860* (New York: The Free Press, c1975), 14–15.

13. Muir apparently recorded this journal entry in one sitting, probably the next day after a refreshing night's sleep. S. Hall Young later reported, with some astonishment, that on the morning after the adventure Muir and the dog climbed a mountain for a better view of the glacier, "and when he returned after nightfall he worked for two or three hours at his notes and sketches." S. Hall Young, *Alaska Days with John Muir*, 196–97.

14. The original journal, each page smudged nearly beyond legibility, is located in the Holt-Atherton Library. The raw transcription that follows, emended only when necessary for clarity, was taken from the 1986 microform edition of the John Muir papers. See AMS journal, August 30, 1880, pp. 41–70, in JMP (microfilm) 26/02114.

15. See chapter 5.

16. John Muir, "Alaska Land," in San Francisco *Daily Evening Bulletin*, 25 September 1880, p. 4, cols. 6–8.

17. See *Alaska Days with John Muir*, and "The Veritable History of Stickine" [1897], AMS 9 pp., in JMP (microfilm) 51/00256.

# Two

# The Telling of "Stickeen"

Muir's career as wilderness advocate coincided with the symbolic close of the frontier and the emergence of an affluent society ready to rethink its relationship to nature.[1] The rise of outdoor recreation as a popular national pastime opened channels of opportunity for both conservationists and preservationists. They took advantage of the more receptive national mood at the close of the nineteenth century to lobby for an end to ruthless exploitation of the nation's natural resources.

Promoting the great outdoors in 1900 was an educational and commercial enterprise largely dependent on newspapers and magazines. Before the 1920s, serials were by far the best, but not the only, form of mass communication. Smaller, but still significant, audiences could be reached by the lecture circuit. In rural areas traveling Chautauqua shows were very popular, but in cities highly promoted individual lectures could draw large crowds, especially if the speaker was a colorful and an effective storyteller.

As both local colorist and naturalist, John Muir met all the qualifications for mass appeal. He had the charisma and talent, if not the desire, to earn a living on the lecture circuit. Conservatively dressed in public despite an untamed beard that he

occasionally trimmed with scissors, he rejected the sartorial gim-
mickry used by some poets and politicians of his day to titillate a
crowd.[2] His voice was firm and emphatic, with a slight hint of
Scotland that he modulated to suit the occasion and the mood.
Among those who were privileged to hear him, his reputation as
teller of fascinating tales vied with his popularity as a nature writer.
Gifford Pinchot said he was "a storyteller in a million."[3]

Yet as public speaker he was a slow starter in a crowd. He
much preferred the comfortable informality of a small circle of
close friends and family to the podium. In his later years, alone in
the Strentzel mansion after his wife died and his children married, he welcomed company and enchanted visitors with stories.
Melville Anderson, an impressionable young Stanford professor
who often came visiting, remembered Muir as a kind of wilderness oracle:

> Scarcely would the guests be seated, when Muir would
> begin, as if thinking aloud, pouring forth a stream of
> reminiscence, description, exposition, all relieved with
> quiet humor, seasoned with pungent satire, starred and
> rainbowed with poetic fancy. What would one not give
> for a phonographic record of those wonderful talks![4]

In more formal settings he appeared reticent, and often had
to be induced or unobtrusively drawn into a conversation. J. E.
Calkins, an unabashed admirer, recalled the time Muir was the
honored guest of his close friend Colonel Alfred H. Sellers, a
wealthy retired Chicago realtor lured to sunny California like
thousands of other health-seekers at the turn of the century. At
his Pasadena mansion he made elaborate preparations to loosen
Muir's tongue. Warning the other guests in advance, Sellers after
dinner started an argument over which way a tree falls when
logged. As the exchange heated up, he innocently asked Muir to

come to his assistance. Muir politely resolved the problem and then, "after a little tactful coaxing along," was soon telling a story that continued into the wee hours:

The company sat there, not speaking or stirring, enchanted by Muir's entrancing periods, till he caught sight of the time and broke off with a sudden "Bless me! I had no idea it was so late." Near 3 o'clock in the morning! "And at that," said Mr. Vroman, "he cut us off too soon. We would have liked him to go on till broad daylight."[5]

Intemperate admiration such as this must be discounted, but fortunately there is corroborating evidence attesting to Muir's ability as a story-teller. David Starr Jordan, president of Stanford, said Muir "always refused to lecture, but to small circles he was a brilliant conversationalist."[6] A voluble talker once he got started, he fascinated his admirers but may have overtaxed the ears of some listeners with long anecdotes. After Muir's visit to Slabsides, John Burroughs said Muir "talks well, but along about two in the morning he gets tiresome. I was a wet rag when he left me."[7]

Of all the anecdotes Muir told over a lifetime of raconteuring, the story of "Stickeen" made the most lasting impression. Its popularity was well established long before it was recorded on paper. Biographer Linnie Marsh Wolfe, interviewing dozens of Muir's relatives and acquaintances, wrote that Muir had told the story to "hundreds of children and grown-ups."[8] Certainly it is the one story most frequently mentioned in the family papers.

Samuel Hall Young, the missionary who accompanied Muir on his two trips to Glacier Bay, was the first to experience the emotional impact of the adventure. It was described to him the day it happened by an exhausted Muir who struggled back to camp in the dark after a seventeen-hour trek with the little dog at his side. After a refreshing rubdown, dry clothes, food, and hot coffee, Muir recounted the day's events in words that left his empathetic companion emotionally drained. Later, Young wrote that he had "listened till midnight, entranced by a succession of vivid descriptions the like of which I have never heard before or since. . . . Before the close of the story Stickeen arose, stepped slowly across to Muir and crouched down with his head on Muir's foot, gazing into his face and murmuring soft canine words of adoration to his god."[9]

Young's narrative, written long after the event, closely resembles the language and characterization Muir employed in his published version and adds little to our understanding of the story. Until Muir asked for a description of the dog's background in 1896, Young never mentioned the dog in several letters to Muir after 1880—a surprising omission if indeed the events following the 1880 adventure transpired as Young's book later proclaimed. One might question his motives for publication. He wanted to enhance Muir's reputation by writing about his Alaskan adventures, but he also had a commercial interest in expanding upon the story after it had become a national bestseller in book form. At any rate Young was given to hyperbole, so his opinions must be used with caution.

A few months after his return from the 1880 trip Muir visited the Magee household. The year previous, Thomas Magee, a San Francisco businessman, and his son Willie had accompanied Muir part way to Alaska. Long after Muir's death Willie remembered hearing the dog story: "While we listened to his vivid description of this great glacier, we were particularly interested in his story of Stickeen, a little dog which accompanied him on a perilous trip across this glacier in a storm, when both nearly lost their lives."[10]

Sarah J. McChesney, an Oakland animal rights activist whose family housed Muir in the winter of 1874 when he first came down from the Sierra to write, recalled seventy years later that he was a reticent talker in those early days but "would go on for hours when started on such interesting stories as *Stickeen*."[11]

Ellen Graydon of Indianapolis, whose family had befriended young
Muir in the 1860s before he left for California, considered his
dog story one of the best examples of his self-sacrificing love for
all of nature's wonders.[12] His niece Cecelia Galloway also mentioned the dog story in her reminiscences:

> I remember my uncle telling stories at our dinner-table,
> and being completely carried away with the thrill of
> them. One that I have heard him tell was afterward
> published in book form,—"Stickeen," the story of the
> little black dog who fell in love with my uncle at first
> sight, and immediately adopted him to be his God
> whom he adored, who followed at his heels all day,
> and slept at his feet at night. The brave little dog who
> shared with him one of the most terrible experiences
> on the great Muir Glacier in Alaska.[13]

Even publication did not satisfy some of Muir's admirers
who wanted to hear it first-hand. After reading the *Century* version, J. E. Calkins and a friend visited Muir at the Martinez ranch
in the fall of 1897. Urging him to expand it into a book, they
were rewarded by a retelling:

> Then he began to tell us that . . . rare tale of icy ad-
> venture, in his own living words. We kept silence while
> he went on, taking his time, weaving that spell of en-
> chantment word by word, with never a moment's hesi-
> tation, to the end. It was 1:30 in the morning when
> we crossed that last abyss, and came off that icy waste,
> and back to earth again . . . [14]

Muir's close friends, the Swetts, must have heard the story
many times. In the mid-1870s Muir wintered at the Swett home
in San Francisco while he worked up his mountain notes for

publication. Never comfortable with "book-making," he sought relief in walking the city streets and in telling stories to the Swett children, Emily, Frank, and Helen.[15]

Stickeen made a lasting impression on Emily Swett Parkhurst, John and Mary's eldest daughter. A talented young writer and journalist who died in 1892 of complications following the delivery of her first child, in the late 1880s she had organized the Pacific Women's Press Association in San Francisco and had become assistant editor of *Californian Illustrated Magazine.* While she was pregnant, she wrote up the story she had heard John Muir tell and sent it to *The Youth's Companion,* a popular weekly journal for young people. Apparently Muir himself knew nothing about Emily's account until it appeared in July of 1893. Geared to youthful readers, it changed the dog's name to "Roger," all but eliminated the descriptive content, exaggerated distances for effect, but otherwise generally followed the essential elements of the adventure. As such it is the first recorded version of Muir's story, and it is reprinted here in its entirety.[16]

## The Yawning Crevasse

*Drawn from the experiences of John Muir, an Alaskan Explorer*

Roger and I left the Indian camp at four o'clock in the morning, in order to have a long day on the glaciers. Roger was a small dog, with a strain of collie blood in his veins. He belonged to the clergyman in our party, but he showed a preference for my company during the whole trip.

For many miles we tramped, stopping once in a while to rest for a moment, or to enjoy the rich glow of color along the edge of the innumerable crevasses where the sun poured through the facets of the disintegrating ice, and caused countless prisms to burst into a blaze of color.

Presently a dark cloud swept across the sky, and in a few moments the snow was falling heavily, while the wind whistled and shrieked fiercely. We beat our way against the storm for some miles, until our progress was stopped by a yawning crevasse some eight feet wide.

We could not retrace our steps; I feared that if we turned back I should lose my bearings. The crevasse must be crossed.

The edges of the chasm were rounding, and as smooth as glass. I could make a running leap of more than eight feet, but if I attempted to leap this gulf, and my heel should glance on the other side, I should be hurled down a thousand feet at least.

Old mountaineer though I was, I was frightened as I looked down at that chasm. Roger, too, felt the danger, and rushed wildly along the banks looking for a better place; but he came back without finding one.

There was nothing to do but jump it. At last I cut a socket for my heel, gaged my distance carefully, and sprang. I tell you a man does not know what elasticity he has until it stands between him and death.

I was successful; and Roger, though frightened, plumped across after me.

For perhaps six miles we pushed on without encountering any serious difficulty. I had just begun to think that we were bearing a little too much to the eastward when I was confronted by a yawning abyss at least forty feet wide. That could not be jumped.

Roger cast an appealing blink up into my face, as much as to say, "Wasn't the last one bad enough, master? Surely you won't risk this?" I bent down and patted him reassuringly, and then we reconnoitered.

For twelve miles, more or less, we followed the bank without finding any way of escape. Then we came to a place where a diagonal sliver of ice spanned the crevasse, but it was six feet below the bank on one side, and the bank rose precipitously fully twenty feet on the other side. It could not be crossed, so we pushed on.

After mile upon mile of labored tramping, I found that we were on an island with but two exits; one by the leap I had taken at first, and which I could not be induced to repeat; the other by that sliver of ice which, as far as I could see, was not over a foot in width, and which came to a sharp edge along the top. It would have been simple enough had the bridge been flush with the banks; but one misstep in the descent of the almost perpendicular incline would have shot us down to death.

Roger could not believe that I would try it. When I had painfully bent over and chipped out the first socket for my heel, his voice rose in bitter lamentations. For a few moments he would wail; then in desperation he would gallop along to see if by some hook or crook there might be a better way that we had overlooked. Shivering and disheartened he would at last return, and falling back on his haunches and tossing his nose up in the air, would renew his howls.

When the last socket had been cut I said to him, "Now, Roger, don't be silly. If I can do it, you can. If we both fail we die together, and God help us."

Roger shrieked dismally.

"I am going over first, Roger," said I, "and I will make the way as easy as I can. So, here goes."

I made the first step. Roger sprang forward to snatch me back by the trousers; but as if realizing the danger of so doing, threw himself suddenly on his haunches and became dumb. Painfully, breathlessly, fearfully I planted my heel in each successive socket, and at last slipped down astride upon that awful sliver of smooth, slippery, treacherous ice.

The cold sweat bathed my brow; I dared not even breathe. I felt as if the falling snowflakes might make me lose my balance. Taking my hatchet from my belt, I proceeded to knock off the top of the ice bridge, leaving a level ribbon on top, not more than three inches across. This was for Roger.

Sixty feet of this; and then before me an almost perpendicular ascent of twenty feet more! When I had reached the other side Roger had set up another continuous howl. I dared not speak to reassure him. Every nerve was strained to the utmost.

How was I to get my feet to the top of the ice bridge without losing my balance?

As high up as I could reach while in the sitting posture I clipped sockets for toes and finger-tips, and near enough together so that Roger could use them. I drew myself up to my feet by my fingertips, and after hours of patient, breathless labor, found myself in a position of safety.

Roger was hoarse with terror. He knew he had to follow me, and yet he would not start.

"Roger," I said, "you must come, and quickly, too. I cannot wait for you; we must get back to camp before night, or we shall freeze as well as starve. Don't be afraid. Put your feet just where mine were."

Roger peered carefully over the edge of the incline. Then, burying his nose between his paws, he howled some more.

"Pah!" I growled, as though disgusted. "I am going. Good-by!"

As I turned on my heel, Roger gave a yelp like a death-knell. Tears were in my eyes. I turned toward him and almost roared:

"Come along! I'll wait."

He braced his little paws together, took the line of direction to the sliver, and with a superhuman effort at self-control, began to slide toward the bridge.

Thank God! the dear little fellow reached it safely. Then such a studied passage across on that three-inch-wide surface!

He seemed to have ceased breathing. One foot was carefully, painfully, slowly pushed out in an exact line with the one already planted—with all the precision of an Indian. I dared not speak, yet I knew he must have heard my heart beat for him.

He was across the sliver; but a horrible straight wall of ice confronted him with overwhelming despair.

"Come, Roger!" I urged. "You must do it. I cannot wait for you all night. I did it; you can. Come, sir, up, up!"

With a sigh that I can never forget he began that upward ascent, digging his nails into the glistening ice with the tension of last despair.

Bravo! he was up at last. When he felt the ground beneath his poor little feet once more, he rushed around two or three times as if bereft of his sense; then leaped at my breast, and my arms closed around him. He yelped, he whined, he cried, he howled, he jumped away from me and rolled over and over in the snow, and then sprang back to my arms. It was the most human expression of joy I have ever seen in an animal. Poor little laddie! I should have hated to leave him behind.

—*Emily Tracy Y. Parkhurst*

No mention of the Parkhurst version has been found in Muir's extant correspondence or notes, so his reaction can only be guessed. Muir may not even have read the Parkhurst story and said nothing out of respect for her memory, although before her death Emily must have informed him of the impending publication. If he read it he probably was more embarrassed than annoyed.[17] Presumably in 1893 Muir still thought of it as a children's story. He told Robert Underwood Johnson he was thinking of working it up for *Knickerbocker Magazine*, but Johnson objected. He wanted it for *Century*.[18]

That summer the had tale reached a wider audience. Muir traveled east, preparing for his first trip abroad with William Keith, who was to join him later. In New York Johnson played host to the hirsute Scot, who wanted to visit the stomping grounds of the New England transcendentalists before sailing. A proto-conservationist and a distinguished member of the eastern literati, Johnson was an ideal traveling companion. He may have heard the story for the first time in Tuolumne Canyon in 1889, when he accompanied Muir on what became the planning trip for the creation of Yosemite National Park.

Muir's eastern visit was intended as a brief stop en route to Europe, but Johnson converted it into a six-weeks' celebrity tour, with Muir as the reluctant debutante. With Johnson opening doors and directing the agenda, Muir found himself the center of attention, a backwoods rustic with a stock of colorful anecdotes. He performed dutifully, meeting the social and intellectual elite, stuffing himself at banquets, and telling stories.

A visit with John Burroughs was one of the first stops on Muir's itinerary. Only a year older, yet in 1893 much better known than Muir, Burroughs was late-nineteenth-century America's most popular nature writer.[19] He was a reluctant host, but at Johnson's insistence he agreed to meet the visiting naturalist at his rustic home near Esopus. Later known by their mutual acquaintances as "The Two Johns," Burroughs and Muir became fond friends despite their contrasting personalities. Muir was an incessant talker whose wiry frame seemed to thrive on nervous energy, quite opposite the portly Sage of Slabsides, who had acquired more conventional sleeping and eating habits.[20] At their first meeting Burroughs was condescending, describing Muir as "an interesting man with the Western look upon him," but a tiring conversationalist. "You must not be in a hurry," he wrote, "or have any pressing duty, when you start his stream of talk and adventure. Ask him to tell you his famous dog story . . . and you get the whole theory of glaciation thrown in."[21]

Moving north to Brahmin country, Johnson and Muir spent several days in and around Boston. They had a delightful day in the company of Thomas Wentworth Higginson, famed author, Civil War colonel of black soldiers, and advocate of women's rights. He escorted them on a Cambridge cultural tour, which included the homes of Lowell and Longfellow, both poets Muir knew well from the books in his personal library. At Harvard Muir was introduced to a number of faculty, including Josiah Royce, the California philosopher, and Francis Parkman, distinguished American historian whose books Muir read avidly. But the man whose work he knew best was Charles S. Sargent, director of the Arnold Arboretum and author of the multi-volume *Silva of North America*.[22] At his home in nearby Brookline, Sargent hosted a banquet with Muir the honored guest. Writing his family later, Muir said he had to repeat the dog story "I don't know how often."[23]

More banquets and story-telling followed. At a dinner party in Manchester, wrote Muir, "Sarah Orne Jewett was there, and all was delightful. Here, of course, Johnson made me tell that dog story as if that were the main result of glacial action and all my studies, but I got in a good deal of ice-work better than this, and never had better listeners."[24]

A quick pilgrimage to Concord highlighted Muir's New England visit. Johnson took him to all the shrines: Concord Bridge, Hawthorne's "Old Manse," the Alcott residence, the graves of Emerson and Thoreau on "Author's Hill" in Sleepy Hollow Cemetery, and, of course, Walden Pond, an easy "saunter" from town. After "a delightful P.M." with Emerson's son Edward Waldo and his father-in-law Judge John S. Keyes, the two visitors caught the night train back to Boston.[25]

The New England tour concluded, Muir and Johnson returned to New York, where a final round of parties and story-telling delayed his departure for Europe. At Gramercy Park Muir dined at the family estate of Gifford Pinchot. In a letter home he described the scene:

> Here and at many other places I had to tell the story of the minister's dog. Everybody seems to think it wonderful for the views it gives of the terrible crevasses of the glaciers as well as for the recognition of danger and the fear and joy of the dog. I must have told it at least twelve times at the request of Johnson or others who had previously heard it. . . . When I am telling it at the dinner tables, it is curious to see how eagerly the liveried servants listen from behind screens, half-closed doors, etc.[26]

The six weeks Muir spent in the East ended with his departure for Europe late in June 1893—without William Keith, who had tired of waiting and sailed alone. But Muir could look back with no small satisfaction: he had mingled with some of the best minds of the continent; he had come as a stranger and had been welcomed as a celebrity, a member of the intellectual elite. Yet like previous westerners who came East in triumph, among eastern literati Muir's popularity as a story-teller tended to overshadow his reputation as a significant writer. Confirmation of his literary skills would have to await the publication in 1894 of his first book, *The Mountains of California.*

In the meantime, the dog story's enthusiastic acceptance stimulated the demand for publication. If describing Stickeen's adventure orally struck such a responsive chord, what might it do in print? Johnson had no doubt it would read just as well as it sounded and by the end of June was already planning for its appearance in *Century* as a colorful anecdote, a thrilling adventure in the Wild West. By 1893, however, Muir had begun to see something more. The eastern tour had heightened his awareness of the dog's potential as a didactic tool. He had little time to develop the thought during the next two years, but as he left for Europe he was already thinking of an expanded version of "Stickeen," a philosophical as well as a physical adventure.

# Endnotes

1. Roderick Nash, *Wilderness and the American Mind,* 3rd ed. (New Haven and London: Yale Univ. Press, c1967, 1982), 141–60.
2. Joaquin Miller's colorful dress set a pattern for local colorists on the lecture circuit. For an example of a mediocre 19th century politician using outlandish costumes to attract a crowd see R. H. Limbaugh, *Rocky Mountain Carpetbaggers: Idaho's Territorial Governors, 1863–1890* (Moscow: University Press of Idaho, c1982), 45–46.
3. Gifford Pinchot, *Breaking New Ground* (Seattle & London: Univ. of Washington Press, c1947, c1972), 103. C. Hart Merriam's reminiscence of the voluble Scot is perhaps the best of many. "To the memory of John Muir," *Sierra Club Bulletin* 10 (January 1917): 146–51.
4. Melville B. Anderson, "The Conversation of John Muir," *The American Museum Journal* XV (March 1915): 118–19.
5. J. E. Calkins, [Reminiscences], unpublished manuscript, ca. 1942, *The John Muir Papers, 1858–1957.* Microform Edition. Ronald H.

Limbaugh and Kirsten Lewis, eds. (Alexandria, VA: Chadwyck-Healey, Inc., 1986), 51/00050, hereafter JMP (microfilm).

6. David Starr Jordan, "John Muir, Naturalist and Poet," *Science* 61 (No. 1588: June 5, 1925): 582.

7. Quoted in Hamlin Garland, "Burroughs the man," *Public Meeting of the American Academy and the National Institute of Arts and Letters in Honor of John Burroughs* (New York: American Academy of Arts and Letters, 1922), 50–51.

8. Linnie Marsh Wolfe, *Son of the Wilderness* (New York: Knopf, 1945), 221.

9. Samuel Hall Young, *Alaska Days with John Muir* (New York: Fleming H. Revell, c1915), 184–88.

10. William A. Magee, "Personal recollections of John Muir," *Sierra Club Bulletin* (Feb. 1936): 25–30.

11. Sarah J. McChesney, Reminiscence of John Muir, unpublished manuscript, 1916, JMP (microfilm), 51/00004.

12. Ellen D. Graydon, [Reminiscence], unpublished manuscript, ca. 1942, JMP (microfilm), 51/00090.

13. Cecelia Galloway, [Reminiscence], unpublished manuscript, 1944, JMP (microfilm), 51/00133. Written long after Muir's death, the details of this anecdote are confused. Galloway obviously had read Young's account of the story and mixed it up with what she remembered from childhood. Young had also mentioned Muir and Stickeen walking on Muir Glacier, but he correctly identified the glacier in Taylor Bay as the site of the adventure, not Muir Glacier as Galloway suggested. William Magee also erroneously named Muir Glacier for the Stickeen incident. William A. Magee, "Personal recollections of John Muir," 30.

14. J. E. Calkins, Reminiscences, ca. 1942, JMP (microfilm), 51/00050, p. 3.

15. Frederick Turner, *Rediscovering America: John Muir in His Time and Ours* (New York: Viking, 1985), 234–35; Margaret Plummer interview, Martinez, California, March 24, 1988; Ruth Sutter phone interview, April 20, 1988.

16. Emilie Tracy Y. Parkhurst, "The Yawning Crevasse," *The Youth's Companion*, 67 (July 13, 1893), 351–52.

17. In the 1897 reminiscence addressed to Muir, S. Hall Young mentioned the Parkhurst version. Referring to the author as a "some lady of

your acquaintance," he said he didn't blame Muir for the dog's unfortunate name change. Muir never mentioned the Parkhurst story in his correspondence or other writings, although Young seemed more curious than upset by the change in the dog's name. See "The Veritable History of Stickine," JMP (microfilm), 51/00256.

18. Muir to Louie Muir, June 13, 1893, as quoted in William F. Badé, *Life and Letters of John Muir*, II (Boston & New York: Houghton Mifflin, 1923), 264–65.

19. Judson D. McGehee, "The Nature Essay as a Literary Genre: an Intrinsic Study of the Works of Six English and American Nature Writers," (Ph.D. Dissertation, Univ. of Michigan, 1958), 27.

20. *The Life and Letters of John Burroughs*, ed. by Clara Barrus, II, 120.

21. Ibid., I, 340, 360.

22. Charles S. Sargent, *The Silva of North America*. 14 v. (Boston: Houghton Mifflin, 1891–1902). Muir's set is missing. Badé's widow later said he had kept it after Muir died. See Edith J. Hadley, "John Muir's Views of Nature and their Consequence" (Ph.D. dissertation, Univ. of Wisconsin, 1956), 167.

23. Muir to Wanda Muir, June 14. 1893, in *Dear Papa: Letters between John Muir and his Daughter Wanda*. Edited by Jean Hanna Clark and Shirley Sargent (Fresno, CA: Panorama West Books, c1985), 36–37; Badé, *Life and Letters of John Muir*, II, 270.

24. Badé, *Life and Letters of John Muir*, II, 271.

25. John S. Keyes, Diary, v. 12, p. 24, June 8, 1893, in Concord Public Library, Concord, Mass.

26. Badé, *Life and Letters*, II, 265–66.

# Three

# The Writing of "Stickeen"

For most of his life Muir kept travel journals, but rarely did he bother to record daily events. On only two known occasions did he keep a diary while he was home. Fortunately for understanding the development of "Stickeen," in both periods he was working on the dog story. Along with his voluminous correspondence, his personal library, and his preliminary draft manuscripts, his diary provides a wealth of data that can help trace the genesis of "Stickeen."

Muir's intent to draft a written version, expressed to Robert Underwood Johnson in 1893, took more than two years to materialize. Back from his European tour in September 1893, Muir devoted his fall and winter months to lobbying on behalf of forestry reserves and the creation of Mount Rainier National Park. Then, for most of 1894, he worked on his first book, *The Mountains of California*, which appeared in October. Between proofing chapters, Muir, at Johnson's urging, drafted and submitted to *Century* an article describing the 1879 discovery of Glacier Bay, the first of three Muir selections on Alaska published by *Century* over the next three years. While fiction was still the magazine's mainstay, since the early 1880s the scope of its content had

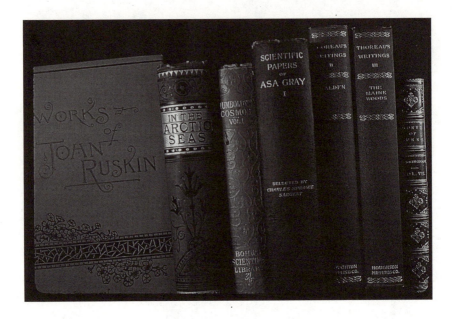

*A selection of books from Muir's personal library.*

expanded under Johnson and his editor-in-chief Richard Watson Gilder.[1]

Both editors had personal as well professional interests in Muir's trips to Alaska. Aside from his conservation efforts, Johnson had developed a warm personal relationship with Muir and his family. Gilder was also a nature enthusiast and, like Johnson, a romantic poet. His brother William H. Gilder, a travelling correspondent for James Gorden Bennett's New York *Herald*, had spent two years in the Arctic with the Schwatka expedition in search of the lost crew of the USS *Jeannette*.[2] In 1881, the year Schwatka and Gilder returned, a government-sponsored sea party aboard the USS *Corwin* also searched for the *Jeannette*. Muir had sailed with them as correspondent for the San Francisco *Bulletin*.

News from the icy northland also made good press in the 1890s. The shrinking-globe school of journalism reached its peak in the *fin de siècle,* when rival magazines and newspapers published the exploits of Fridtjof Nansen, Robert E. Peary, Roald Amundsen, and other polar pioneers, still years away from their ultimate discoveries. Muir had no apparent polar pretensions, but the popularity of his newspaper reports from the margins of *terra incognita* nevertheless excited his *Century* editors, who pressed him for a series of articles on Alaska, including the dramatic story of "Stickeen," which Johnson wanted in Muir's "liveliest style."[3]

Muir intended to begin on the dog story as soon as the article on the discovery of Glacier Bay was finished, but Johnson sidetracked what Muir called the "Canis" project by asking for revisions to the initial submission. He wanted Muir to describe the glacier named after him in greater detail. Muir's response was to propose a separate article entitled "Adventures on the Muir Glacier." After this second narrative, he wrote, he would give *Century* "a short article on the dog story in all its far reaching glory!"[4]

The tone of Muir's early remarks, as well as Johnson's letters, make clear that initially neither considered the dog story very substantive. The magazine editor recognized its obvious entertainment value: it was a simple but dramatic tale with deep emotional impact. With only minor editorial tinkering it could be shaped to meet the conventions of popular taste: high excitement, linear development, dramatic description, an element of piety, extreme danger, and a happy ending. Its setting in the Wild West might offer an exotic escape to readers ambivalent about the psychic consequences of progress in the machine age.[5] Potentially, at least, it contained many of the standard props of contemporary formula fiction: an untamed frontier, spectacular scenery, and colorful characters who followed conventional moral guidelines. As Nina Baym has noted, those standards in Victorian fiction included individual differentiation of characters based on "inner traits that are expressed in outer actions," internal consistency among those traits, and characterization that revealed the particular moral qualities of each character.[6] It also might exhibit in a true story what Victorian convention often required in fiction: a mystery that leads to unexpected events and a discovery of hidden forces at work, usually attributed to Providence.[7] "Stickeen" thus had nearly an ideal cast to suit the times: noble savages, a pious missionary, a soft-hearted hero with a gruff exterior, and a small, "worthless" dog that under extraordinary circumstances revealed hidden, near-human, moral, and intellectual qualities.

All this in a single story, told with the emphatic spontaneity of an eyewitness! Surely the tale that flowed so naturally from the teller's lips could quickly be set to paper. Both Johnson and Muir thought so in 1894. But the two other articles on Alaska came first, and they took more time than anticipated.

It was early February of the following year before Muir finished revising the "Discovery" article. To his diary he complained: "It seems strange that a paper that reads smoothly & may be finished in ten minutes should require months to write."[8] A week later, hard at work on the second Alaska narrative, published in *Century* in August of 1897 as "The Alaska Trip," Muir took time out for a more extended self-criticism:

> Am making slow head way with my literary task. The hardest of all work to me. It is so difficult to say things that involve thought at once clearly & attractively— to make the meaning stand out through the words like a fire on a hill so that all must see it without looking for it. Yet this is what the times demand in magazine work.[9]

Despite his complaint, the second piece was finished in two weeks. "Now for the minister's dog & Adventures on the Muir Glacier," he noted on February 22.[10]

To begin the narrative, Muir first revised his 1880 notes.[11] The text of this notebook shows clearly that the dog was incidental to the events on Taylor glacier. Indeed, not until after he completed a revised account of the August 30 excursion did he go back and insert references to Stickeen. In describing his efforts to cross the glacier, for example, he first wrote that "Many a mile I thus traveled," then revised the line to read "Many a mile Stick & I thus had to travel. . . ."[12] His explanation for cutting off the tops of ice bridges also changed in this narrative. In the first version he cut them because "they were narrow & sharp like knifeblades" which "compelled" him "to straddle them & grip with my knees cutting off these edges as I progressed." Later he lined that sentence out and penciled in a new explanation: he cut them "so Stick[een] could follow, & he did follow without once showing fear or even reasonable caution."[13]

At every opportunity while this work proceeded, he immersed himself in his books. The bulk of Muir's working library, a well-exercised—even dog-eared before restoration—collection of some 1,250 volumes, he acquired after 1880, when home, family, wealth, and more time for reading made book acquisition and storage practical. The literary core contain much of the best of late eighteenth- and nineteenth-century British and American literature, poetry, science, philosophy, and history. More than forty percent are covered with holographic marginalia and endnotes that point like psychic roadmaps to Muir's reading interests and sources of inspiration. The quantity and quality of this handwritten evidence is unusually rich compared to the extant libraries of other famous literary figures.[14]

The stress of increased responsibilities following his father-in-law's death in 1890 weighed heavily on him until relatives came to his assistance.[15] He read in part to escape the daily grind of ranching and "book-making." But he also read for ideas and inspiration. There is a close correlation between his reading patterns and the evolution of the narrative. Within a factual framework built upon the notes of his 1880 trip, he wove in threads of description, characterization, and evaluation adapted from the books of his library.

This conscious effort to mold the narrative by digesting and building upon ideas and words from the writings of others is called "research" in the scholarly world. It is an essential part of the writer's trade, especially in the production of academic dissertations and other forms of nonfiction, but also in historical fiction and even in substantive dramatic works or poetry. Indeed, almost all literary production is crafted in part from the work of predecessors. It is therefore no surprise that Muir's literary output is partly derivative. What is unusual, however, is the degree to which Muir searched other writings, both fictional and nonfictional, for ideas to aid in the drafting of "Stickeen." And what is wholly uncharacteristic of other western writers is his systematic effort to compose parts of the dog story using the endpages of books in his personal library.[16]

The evidence for this extraordinary procedure can be found in over one hundred volumes of his book collection.[17] These volumes became a primary source of ideas, as well as a medium of expression. Whenever he found a passage or a line of text of particular interest he would turn to the blank pages at the back of the book and jot down a note, a phrase, or sometimes a comment. On other occasions while reading and thinking about the dog, an idea would strike him that he wanted to record in the back of the book, whether or not it had anything to do with the book's content. In a five-year period he filled over 250 pages in the backs of at least 105 books with such thoughts. His reading complicated the composition by filling his mind—and his pen—with words and ideas he tried to incorporate into the narrative.

When he began to use his books to write down a personal story he had told many times before cannot be determined

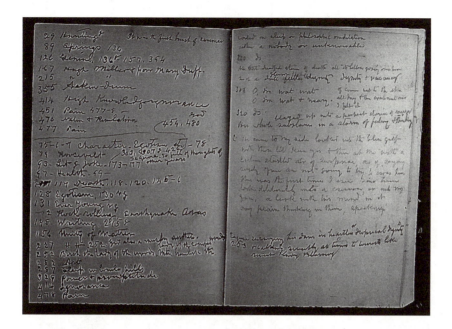

*A page of Muir notes on the endpages of* Horem Subsecum
*by John Brown.*

·precisely, but a rough sequence can be deduced from external evidence. Muir never bothered to date his correspondence or manuscript drafts, much less the notes he wrote in the backs of books. S. Hall Young remembered, after Muir died, that in 1897 Muir had said "that he had been thinking of the story all of these years and jotting down paragraphs and sentences as they occurred to him."[18] The comment implies that Muir had been working on the story since 1880, but it is unlikely that he did much note-taking before 1892, the year he acquired a three-volume edition of John Brown's *Horae Subsecivae* ("Hours of Leisure"). A handwritten note on the endpages of volume two indicates that this set was most likely the first in which Muir recorded notes on the dog story.

A Scottish physician with literary inclinations, Brown was widely read in Britain and the United States in the late-Victorian era. The three volumes of *Horae* are Brown's collected works, an anthology of writings gathered from previous publications. In volume two was a short version of his most memorable essay, a dog story, "Rab and His Friends," first published in 1858.[19] Muir may have been familiar with it before 1892, but in that year a fellow-Scotsman and soul-mate, William Keith, gave him the three-volume edition of *Horae*.[20]

"Rab" may have started Muir thinking seriously about recording his own dog story. Brown's reminiscence tells of lifelong kinship between a drayman and his dog, a huge old mastiff, graying and scarred from street fights but devoted to his human family. Narrated in the first person by the author, who was just beginning his practice when the incident occurred, the story ends tragically in the death of all principal characters, including the dog. The reprint in *Horae* is devoid of Muir marginalia or notes, but from it Muir must have learned the value of humanizing the four-legged subject of the story.

Brown's other essays in *Horae* also had a strong, if indirect, influence on Muir's composition. The two separate sets of endnotes in each volume demonstrate that Muir first read *Horae* cover to cover, then went back a second time, selectively reading and noting words and passages that he associated with some action or event from his own 1880 adventure. Both these readings must have been completed before his 1893 trip East, when the first clamor arose to write down "Stickeen" for publication in *Century*. If so, it was useful preparation for his 1893 celebrity tour, for he was called on time and again to repeat the story. Having worked it out on paper must have aided in the telling, while apparently not diminishing the listener's belief in the teller's spontaneity.

One handwritten passage in volume two of *Horae* fortuitously provides a date for the writing by noting that "12 yrs have gone [since the 1880 adventure] but I now see that awful gulf & the bridge & I see Stick[een] his wild eyes hear his agonizing crys see his little feet his mind working his hysterical joy of deliverance." That passage also helps date an upgraded version that Muir transcribed to the pages of a notebook in 1896. There he began with the same wording but caught the error and changed "12" to "16."[21]

The ten pages of notes that Muir took while reading *Horae* form a rough first draft of the dog manuscript. In two of the three volumes Muir began to extend his notes into bits and pieces of narrative—desultory and fragmentary, but still recognizable as part of the dog story. He made many attempts to describe the dog's character, the hardest part of the story to get just right. He began the task by stringing together short passages loaded with descriptive adjectives and alliterative phrases. Old and new metaphors intermingled with spontaneous associations in a disorderly layering of words like piles of paper on his desk. Before the "great trial day," "Stickeen" was "outrageously tranquil": "calm as a bowlder or on a hilltop fringed with daisies." "Like one of those little plump squat unshakable cactuses he could keep calm & fat in any desert without care and make his way thro any wind his hair unruffled like a salmon through swift water." Yet at the moment of crisis, the dog "became a perfect pact of misery," "canish and comprehensible." Then he crossed the ice bridge and was "Pluckt out of the very jaws of death."[22]

Some of Muir's associations he borrowed directly from Brown's text. Whereas Brown describes a classic pose of Bonaparte, who "set his face against the heavens," Muir has Stickeen "set his face against storms cold like Nap[oleon]." When Brown, in an essay on Henry Vaughan, concludes with a quotation—"Out of the eater comes forth meat; out of the strong comes forth sweetness"—Muir extends the maxim in an endnote with a rhetorical query about Stickeen—"But what comes out of dullness[?]" In a footnote to the essay on Vaughan, Brown refers to a

"Fairy Legend" of the "Pwcca" that sits on a milestone by the roadside, an "odd little fellow" with a "certain forlorn dignity and meek sadness. . . . What is he? and whence? Is he surface or substance? Is he smooth and warm? Is he glossy, like a black-berry?" Muir lined the passage with a pencil mark and used parts of it to describe Stickeen. "Smooth & glossy as a berry," he wrote on a back page, later expanding that to "Shining like a black-berry & as silent[,] brim full of meek dull sadness & the dignity of dullness." The "berry" metaphor survived several later drafts but had disappeared by the final submission.

Muir also tried to find the right words to develop the one-ness uniting dogs and men. "What an opening that little d[og] made for me through the dark that separates us from the count-less multitudes of fellow speechless mortals," he wrote. The gla-cial "trial like white light laid the mind & soul bare." In the "dreadful crevasse" he "saw down into the depths thru Stick[een], of our common nat[ure]." This was the fundamental message that took its author months, even years, to develop fully.

The habits of note-taking and phrase-making he demon-strated on the back pages of *Horae* Muir repeated time and again over the next few years in dozens of other books in his library. The pattern varies widely, depending on the content of each book and the circumstances in which it was used, yet there is an overall consistency and coherence that shows a progressive evolution of thought and language. These are not random, haphazard efforts to flesh out a story, but a systematic effort to fuse original ideas into familiar English prose style.

Though they vary widely by author and type, over half of the volumes Muir used in writing "Stickeen" were written by three of his favorite authors: Thomas Carlyle, Nathaniel Hawthorne, and Sir Walter Scott. Muir's interest in these writers began as early as his teenage years. By the late 1870s he had read several volumes by each, and at his first opportunity, he purchased full sets of all three.

Carlyle was a continual source of ideas while Muir worked on the "Canis" project. Although forty years younger, the American Scot emulated the moral and metaphysical views of his elder countryman. Both believed in a purposive universe guided by the hand of an immanent, omnipotent, majestic creator-god. Both were radical critics of nineteenth-century Christianity, attacking what they regarded as false icons of institutional religion that had corrupted the divine message and alienated humanity from its true mission. Both believed that the progressive materialism of the modern age represented a decline of Christian morality. Both saw eternal truths in the book of nature, a manifestation of divine love.[23]

Muir poured over each of the thirty-four volumes of Carlyle in his library, marking selected passages, indexing certain ideas, and in some cases modeling his style after Carlyle's prose. In volume one of *Critical and Miscellaneous Essays*, for example, Muir marked Carlyle's description of Johann August Müsaeus, an eighteenth-century German author: "for his heart was gay and kind; and an imperturbable good-humor, more potent than a panoply of brass, defended him from the stings and arrows of outrageous Fortune to the end of his pilgrimage." In an endnote Muir wrote: "(Canis) 321 imperturbable good humor or good dullness protected him like a suit of brazen armor from the stings & arrows of outrageous fortune. . . . "[24] That particular sentence never reached advanced draft stage, although others in the dog story evolved out of ideas originally found in Carlyle.

In the final draft of "Stickeen," for example, Muir described the dog's reaction to the realization that he had to cross the ice bridge: "one could see the works of his mind like the movements of a clock out of its case." That passage alone took Muir over four years of reflection and modification. Its history is convoluted and impossible to trace in a chronological progression. It may have begun with Muir's reading of Hugh Miller's *Life and Letters*. He received the two-volume set in 1872 as a gift from "I.

Hall" of New York, probably Isaac Hollister Hall, a New York attorney and oriental scholar, and later curator of the Metropolitan Museum of Art. In the second volume Muir marked a passage in which a Dr. McCosh recollects Miller's "brilliant" conversation "when there were only a few persons present"— precisely the kind of audience Muir preferred. McCosh said one could see Miller's "thoughts laboring in his brain as distinctly as you see the machinery in a clock when the clock-work is in a glass case."[25]

The "clock" passage could also have evolved out of the Miller text combined with a passage in volume two of Carlyle's *Critical and Miscellaneous Essays*. The holograph entries suggest that Muir read the volume, or at least selections, two or three times, but in what sequence or when is not possible to determine. Almost certainly he was reading it in the early 1890s, since the "Canis" notes are an integral part of Muir's holographic text. In the printed text Muir found an essay on his favorite poet, Robert Burns, in which Carlyle described the Scot's use of nature as a source of poetic imagery: "The mysterious workmanship of a man's heart, the true light and the inscrutable darkness of man's destiny, reveal themselves not only in capital cities and crowded saloons, but in every hut and hamlet where men have their abode." Muir's endnote metamorphosed the passage: "(Canis) Like a clock out of its case Stickeen was revealed & we could see the work-manship of a dogs heart a thing as mysterious as man's, for when both are infinite how shall we measure them."[26]

But the passage took a different twist in the back pages of volume six of Carlyle's *History of Frederick II*, which Muir seemed to have used for draft paper for the "Stickeen" text before he actually read the book. The first holographic entry in a flowing hand begins in midsentence: "one could see through his troubled mind as if he were a piece of ice with sunshine streaming thro it."[27] That variant did not take root, however. In the holograph endnotes in Scott's *Fortunes of Nigel*, which Muir also apparently used as draft paper before he read the text, the earlier version of the clock metaphor appears with only minor alterations.[28] It also appears in substantially the same form on the back pages of Hawthorne's *Scarlet Letter,* which contains nearly three pages of "Stickeen" text in Muir's flowing longhand.[29] These latter variants he eventually transferred from endnotes to a notebook for easier reference as the composition took form.

An uncased clock was the kind Muir made as a youthful inventor in Wisconsin. His reading at midlife evoked memories of an earlier era before the thousand-mile walk, when his psychic energies were devoted to industry and mechanics. By midcentury, clocks were the industrial icons of Yankee-Puritan culture, material symbols of orderly progress and control over nature.[30] In his 1869 journal, published later as *My First Summer in the Sierra,* he said he felt sorry for his friends from the lowlands who were "bound by clocks, almanacs, orders, duties, etc."[31] Nearly thirty years later he saw still a different vision through the lens of experience and the transcendental prose of Carlyle and Miller. In metaphorically looking at the inner works of clocks and men and dogs, Muir saw through the exposed physical parts to the common spiritual essence within. Exploring the stirrings of Stickeen's heart followed popular taste in late Victorian fiction. Nina Baym found an increasing tendency after 1850 to address the "interior life" of fictional characters. Literary reviewers condemned works that seemed shallow and superficial in characterization. In contrast, those that analyzed the "more subtle and refined vibrations of the soul" were praised for "psychological" insight along the lines of *The Scarlet Letter* and *Jane Eyre.* One reviewer, touting the writings of American novelist Emma Southworth, said she had "keen insight into the workings of the human heart"—words nearly identical to those found in Carlyle and Muir.[32]

Muir's library also contains two complete sets of Scott's works in separate editions. The earliest was evidently published in 1876, although Muir may have acquired it after that date.

Every volume in the Waverley series of this edition is filled with two to four pages of handwritten notes, many relating to "Stickeen." In some cases two or three separate note sequences are evident, showing that Muir returned more than once to these favorites that he first began to read as a teenager. The note patterns in these volumes resemble those found in most of the books by Carlyle. A few notes bear some relationship to the printed text, but most are entirely independent, as if Muir disassociated himself from Scott's narrative and let his mind drift from one idea to another in a kind of intellectual day-dreaming. In almost every case, the drafts of the "Stickeen" text appear in the endpapers before any other notes, signifying that while reading this particular edition Stickeen weighed heavily on Muir's mind. He must have read these particular volumes in the early nineties, sometime after working up his notes in *Horae*, but before commencing to transpose his notes in 1896. Sometime—perhaps years—after recording his notes on "Stickeen" in the Scott volumes, he went back over them and prepared page indices to other topics of interest.

Scott's evocative word combinations directly influenced the phraseology of the "Stickeen" text. Muir borrowed ideas from Scott to generate lines of text intended for his own manuscript, gradually working them down to a word or two in the final draft. One surviving idea was the dog's "triumphant joy" upon reaching the other side of the crevasse. It started with a sentence in *Old Mortality*, where Scott mentions on page 19 the "joyous burst which attends the dismissing of a village school on a fine summer evening." Muir's endnote reads: "19 Stickeen burst of joy triumphant." The idea evolved into a line in the final draft of 1897 reflecting on Stickeen's behavior after the ordeal: "Never before or since have I seen anything like so passionate a revulsion from fear to uncontrollable, triumphant joy."

Most of these long sentences were completely transformed by secondary and tertiary revisions in later drafts. In *Fair Maid of*

*Perth*, for example, Muir could associate the heroine's impending doom with the dog's predicament: "The assembly rose to receive the melancholy group, and saluted them with an expression of the deepest sympathy, which Magdalen, though the mate of poor Oliver, returned with an air of dignity, which she borrowed, perhaps, from the extremity of her distress." In his endnote Muir had another thought: "Had the danger been less the distress [would have] been ludicrous." The same reflection, slightly modified, found its way into the final draft as Stickeen confronted the crevasse: "Had the danger been less his distress would have seemed ridiculous."[33]

The Muir library's edition of Hawthorne's complete works carries an 1884 publication date, but Muir had read selected volumes much earlier, and during the years he was working on the "Stickeen" draft he went back to this New England novelist. Hawthorne and Scott had much in common, the latter deeply influencing the former just as both influenced Muir. The pattern of Muir's endnotes in Hawthorne's works resembles those in Carlyle and Scott. Occasionally, however, reading Hawthorne brought out a more philosophical Muir. In *The Blithedale Romance*, for instance, a sentence on the character of women raised a point Muir associated with Stickeen. Hawthorne's text: "[Women] are not natural reformers, but become such by the pressure of exceptional misfortune." Muir's endnote response transformed the New Englander's idea into an aphorism: "We never know until tried what is in us. In stress of mortal danger in our own or others behalf we do what under other calm common moods appears utterly impossible, & therefore tried souls always wonder more at themselves than at others."[34]

This statement never reached the final draft, but other ideas abstracted from Hawthorne did. One of the most important was the idea of latency. Muir readily accepted the implications of natural selection,[35] but how to translate the significance of common ancestry into popular parlance challenged Muir and other writers in the Darwinian age. An idea came to him after reading a passage in volume one of *Our Old Home*, which discussed the American penchant to engage in wishful thinking about having royal ancestry. Hawthorne ridiculed the notion: "There is no estimating or believing, till we come into a position to know it, what foolery lurks latent in the breasts of very sensible people. . . . " Muir liked the passage and modified it for the "Stickeen" text. "There is no estimating or believing," his endnote reads, "what wisdom & sentiment lurks latent in our lower relations until made manifest by some great experience."[36] Again, the statement never made it to Muir's final draft, but the idea did, although cut down by his editor to a couple of metaphorical expressions.

As Muir's outdoor pace quickened in the spring of 1895, his writing schedule suffered accordingly. But it was not spring fever that kept him from lifting his pen. The Strentzel ranch demanded his attention. Scaled down by subdividing and subletting since the death of his father-in-law in 1890, it was still too large and complex to let others manage without continual oversight.

Muir's diary for the first six months of 1895 documents a psychic conflict between promise and performance as he struggled with the double burden of domestic and literary responsibilities. The work ethic tugged at his Calvinist conscience. Early in April, preoccupied with "killing weeds and plowing," he took a few notes and read, but otherwise did "but little in a literary way."[37] One sunny Monday he spent "in reading but alas! not a sentence of composition & so I feel at fault."[38] All the next day, too, he read: "this I can do always from morn till night & never weary— but composition, the devil seems to keep me from it—though I feel that my day of life is fast speeding away & that I must tell my story to the world."[39]

The same theme is repeated over and over in later entries, coupled with a yearning for escape:

[April 24:] Very little literary work being done. The Ranch affairs and those of the family bid fair to wreck it utterly—O for a lodge . . .

[April 25:] How the time flies, & how little of my real work I accomplish in the midst of all this ranch work & the petty details of a domestic kind. How grand would be a home in a hollow Sequoia![40]

May and June presented new diversions: business trips to San Francisco; visitors and visitations; correspondence that accumulated faster than he could respond; short hikes with his daughters over "Mt. Wanda" and "Mt. Helen," two nearby hills on the coast range. But always the ranch work hanging over his head until he could stand it no longer. With his wife Louie's blessing, he promised himself a summer trip.[41]

He made some effort to draft "Stickeen" in between frustrations, but the work went badly. A laconic note to Johnson in June said it all: "Have been trying the dog story—a tough job."[42] It was much easier to read and take notes. The *Century* editor tried to be helpful, suggesting in reply: "You ought to have a stenographer hidden behind a screen while you tell that dog story!"[43]

That dogs remained on his mind is clear from an April diary entry on the death of Pedro, a terrier killed by poisoned bread intended for rats in a packing house. He reflected on the incident: "I loved Pedro—so wise & affectionate—he belonged to a neighbor & I saw him nearly every day. A rough wiry-ha[i]red fellow—homely but of such is I hope the Kingdom of heaven."[44] About the same time he clipped two book notices from the papers and filed them in an envelope labeled "books to buy." The books were *The Nature & Development of Animal Intelligence*, by Wesley Mills, and *Our Friend the Dog*, by Maurice Maeterlinck.[45] Neither book appears on the 1915 inventory, but they may have disappeared from his library before he died.

The "Canis" project stopped abruptly in July when he left for the high Sierra. It took eighteen months to get back to it. Most of that time he was preoccupied with travel and politics. His 1895 summer in the mountains renewed his spirit but physically took its toll. Five weeks of hiking on a meagre diet, without bedroll or a coat, might tax the energy of even the most vigorous fifty-seven-year-old. That fall and winter Muir and Johnson and other Sierra Club members lobbied for recession of Yosemite Valley to federal management as part of the surrounding national park. Since 1864 the valley had been in the state's custody. They also rallied to defend President Cleveland's forestry reserves from conservatives and the lumber lobby in Washington. It was time-consuming but of inestimable importance in bringing public attention to conservation issues and in building the momentum for a comprehensive review of the nation's forest resources. The following year a presidential commission was appointed for that purpose, with Muir serving as unofficial advisor.

"Stickeen" returned to his conscience intermittently during this long period. He found a little time in the winter and spring of 1895–1896 to "peg away" at the story,[46] mostly by more reading and note-taking, but about the same time he began transferring his notes from earlier readings into a blue notebook for easy reference. Passage by passage, line by line, he scoured the accumulated jottings in the backs of the books he had read, copying out phrases and sentences and sometimes whole paragraphs. For the first eighty pages he lifted notes nearly verbatim from about forty books, some of which he had read for the first time after 1892, others of which he had read earlier but now went back over to mark passages relevant to the story or to draft sentences based on earlier readings.[47] He edited as he worked, altering syntax, adding or removing text, changing the diction to sharpen a point or to clarify meaning. C. Hart Merriam said much of Muir's writing "time was spent in balancing, paragraphing, and arranging" text for publication. "He possessed a surprising amount of literary acumen," said Merriam, "and usually cut out and trimmed down much that he had written, saying it was a serious error to dwell too long on one detail; that the reader wearied of a single theme and should be led along by frequent changes . . . ."[48]

In the last twenty pages of the notebook he began revising earlier entries into coherent passages that could be used later. Sometime after he filled the notebook, he went back over it as he did with his journals, preparing a topical index on the back page that shows the organization of the story slowly taking form. The index includes page listings for "advance of gl[acier]", "setting out," "on the gl," "on the brink of crevasse," "escape," "study of animals," "upshot," "return to camp," "caution," and other topics.

The "very slow headway" that he reported to Johnson in the spring of 1896 continued to worry his editor. "I hope the charm of that dog story will not be eliminated in the stifleness of print," replied Johnson, repeating for the third time his suggestion to "tell it to somebody in the presence of a stenographer."[49] But Muir was too busy to heed the advice. He managed to write his old companion S. Hall Young, asking him for information on the dog's background,[50] but then set aside the story to work on more pressing matters. That summer he spent three months on the road traveling with commission members after a month in the East and a three-week dash to Alaska, his fifth since 1879.

Between trips he found time to work on a backlog of writing projects based on earlier excursions. Most important were two articles on forest conservation, one for *Harper's Weekly* and the other for *The Atlantic Monthly*.[51] Yet "Stickeen" still beckoned. "I mean to tackle that old dog story soon," he wrote Johnson late in October, after his return to Martinez.[52]

Finally in January 1897, with the ranch work in a winter lull, he took up his pen in earnest. He wrote a reminder to Young; sometime in late January or early February, he received a reply to his inquiry of the previous year. Young apologized for the delay, blaming it on poor postal service.[53] Included in his letter was a lengthy reminiscence, an important document in reconstructing the literary history of "Stickeen." Some of the characterization and several physical details in Muir's final story originated with the missionary. Young remembered that the dog had "glossy, silky hair" that hung almost to the ground. He was "useless" as a work dog, but he was full of fun and had "good looks" that set him apart from other animals. Young reminded Muir of the dog's irritating habit of missing the boat, swimming to catch up so he could be hauled aboard, then waiting to shake off the water until he got between Muir's legs. Muir did not use that line, nor the reminder that he had kicked out at the dog more than once, never hurting the animal but giving him fair notice of his displeasure. Indeed, said Young, Stickeen's biggest triumph was winning over the grouchy Scot, who had first thought the dog totally useless and a nuisance.[54]

Spurred by new information about the dog's background from his old friend,[55] Muir worked feverishly for the next six months. The story still had to be sandwiched between polishing off the articles on forestry and parks for *Harper's Weekly* and *The Atlantic Monthly,* a lengthy book review, and continued lobby efforts on behalf of forest reserves and Yosemite recession. Nevertheless, he sensed that the end was near for the "Canis" manuscript, and he drove himself forward.

Muir had run out of room in the blue notebook by this time, so he began a second notebook using a lined school tablet. Following the same technique he had used earlier, he transcribed selected notes from the earlier notebook into this one, editing and polishing as he wrote. Some of the tablet notes came directly from endnotes he had jotted down on the backpages of his books. As the school tablet filled, familiar fragments of the final draft began to appear. Still it was not a complete narrative; the next step was to write out a full draft on single sheets of bond paper, pulling sentences and phrases out of the tablet as he worked. If he decided to change a sentence or paragraph, he would either insert the revision above the original line, or write out a new page with the insertion integrated into the new text. The old page he tossed on a stock pile of leaves that could be used again on the blank side—a standard procedure, for Muir never threw any old notes or draft pages away. After his death the accumulated residue of his cast-off drafts remained with his papers and eventually came to the Holt-Atherton Library with the rest of his papers. They show a progressive evolution of style and substance as the story unfolded.

Drafting a narrative was not just a matter of transcribing and editing earlier notes, however. The story was too complicated for that. He wanted to incorporate the conceptual models he had struggled to develop since 1880, and they required reviewing his booknotes as well as absorbing new ideas from books recently purchased. As the notes in John Brown's *Horae* demonstrate, one idea Muir initially wanted to incorporate came from the writings of the eighteenth-century Swedish scientist and theologian Emanuel Swedenborg. Intellectuals and artists were beguiled by his primitivism, his antisectarianism, his theory of natural harmonies of body, mind and spirit, and his belief in reincarnation—ideas which might sound familiar to New Age mystics today.[56] The evidence of Swedenborgian ideas in "Stickeen" comes from Muir's holograph notes in *Horae Subsecivae*, the John Brown trilogy that William Keith had given him in 1892. Keith had delved deeply into Swedenborgianism after becoming friends with Joseph Worcester, pastor of northern California's second Swedenborgian church.[57] The Scottish painter may have been the reason Muir, over a thirty-year period, acquired several Swedenborgian books for his personal library. His interest was not as deep as Keith's, but he had read Emerson's essays, as well as the book Emerson had sent him in 1871 written by another American Swedenborgian, Sampson Reed.[58] Swedenborg's depiction of extra-sensory perception probably intrigued Muir more than his theology.[59] Yet the handwritten notes in the volumes by Brown show that Swedenborg's mystic teachings, especially the "correspondences" among man, nature, and spirit, were on Muir's mind as he struggled with the compositional and philosophic elements of "Stickeen."

Sometime between 1892 and early 1895, in the back of volume one of *Horae Subsecivae*, Muir wrote: "Stick[een] like Swedenborg a herald of a new gospel." Later—probably in the winter of 1895–1896, while he was "pegging away" at the story— he transferred the early ideas he had written to the blue-bound notebook that became his first collection of phrases and ideas for "Stickeen." Omitting the direct reference to Swedenborg, he wrote: "Stick was the herald of a new gospel." This phrase he revised a third time in the spring of 1897, when his second notebook, the school tablet, evolved from the work he had done earlier. Now the line read: "To me he was the herald of a new gospel—a new evangel—& to me this little Alaskan d[og] became immortal." But Muir was still dissatisfied. The same notebook shows at least two further efforts to redraft the same sentence.[60] He continued to polish the line as he moved from notebook to draft text, but as he did so the stylistic demands of the text outweighed the expository intent. In subsequent drafts the "herald of a new gospel" and other allusions to the Swedish mystic disappeared.[61]

Latency was a more important idea still not worked into the narrative. Muir had roughed out some sentences, but not yet was the concept in a shape he could use in a popular magazine. The theme kept surfacing in his reading, as in Hawthorne's *Marble Faun*, where "Kenyon, as befitted the professor of an imaginative art, was endowed with an exceedingly quick sensibility, which was apt to give him intimations of the true state of matters that lay beyond his actual vision." Muir's endnote expanded this statement into a sermon on latency and oneness:

> Never was a warm heart more completely hopelessly hidden than in this little dull d[og]—a heart so brimming full of quick human sensibility. Never one so fully revealed, & but for this supreme peril he might have lived & died unknown. Now all his widely varied tribes are redeemed from the judgment of death & have taken their place with man in all his hopes & fears[,] earthly & heavenly[,] in this world & the next. I had long felt in a dim uncertain way that we all[,] man & beast[,] were one, flowing from one f[oun]t[ai]n, now it is no longer dim. Children of one father."[62]

Though Muir worked on this theme in many passages, the final draft included only two references to latent powers and oneness. Both were expressed metaphorically. One was the clock metaphor, discussed earlier. The second may also have originated from a passage in Carlyle, although its precise lineage is obscure. The final paragraph of the 1909 version of "Stickeen"—a version Muir completed in 1897 and partly resurrected after Johnson's radical surgery—contains a well-honed expression of Muir's debt to the dog: "I have known many dogs, and many a story I could tell of their wisdom and devotion; but to none do I owe so much as to Stickeen . . . through him as through a window I have ever since been looking with deeper sympathy into all my fellow mortals."[63]

Muir may have lifted the expression from volume three of *Critical and Miscellaneous Essays*. Carlyle had written in an essay on Schiller: "There is properly no object trivial or insignificant; but every finite thing, could we look well, is as a window, through which solemn vistas are opened into infinitude itself."[64] Muir marked the passage in the margin, but no paraphrase appears in the endnotes. In the first volume of Brown's *Horae Subsecivae*, however, Muir wrote: "Eyes little windows opening into a lighter interior of soul." It is possible Muir read Brown before Carlyle, but the tone and texture of different pencil notes and marks show that he reread or at least returned to favorite volumes over extended periods. The precise early development of his window metaphor is therefore impossible to discern.

From his notes in *Horae* Muir wrote into his 1896 notebook: "Eyes became windows opening into a mind & soul."[65] About the same time, he read the *Listener in the Country* by Joseph Edgar Chamberlin. A Chicago journalist and dog-lover, Chamberlin claimed in a chapter entitled "The Good of Dogs" that associating with pets as a child "tends to make one lighter-hearted, more good-natured, more friendly and serene."[66] Prompted by these remarks, Muir in the back of the book revised his window metaphor: "Stick[een] a window thro wh I see all the animal kingdom." A later page of his 1896 notebook reformulated the passage: "dull & colorless—still became to me a window {opening into the depths of animal kingdom}"[67] Several pages later he again reworked it to read: "He was a window that let me see down into the depths of animal nature."[68] His final draft for *Century* in 1897 had still another version, quoted two paragraphs above. The entire passage was one of the "digressions" Johnson deleted, but Muir brought it back in the 1909 book publication of *Stickeen*.

This textual surface shifting as the composition evolved reveals both superficial stylistic alterations as well as profound psychic struggles that complicated the writing process. Johnson wanted a simple descriptive narrative, just the way he remembered Muir telling it. But Muir realized that was no longer enough. As a free-lance writer for a popular magazine, he was bound by the prescriptive guidelines of its editor, but he wanted to educate as well as entertain. Education meant treading new ground, moving beyond the confines of the nature essay into story-telling. Instead of merely describing a past event, he had to take liberties with the facts for the sake of the plot. At the same time he wanted to explore recent philosophical issues raised by the implications of Darwinism. His reading and reflection since 1880 had sharpened his thinking about animals and their role in nature, and as he labored, he probed deeper into philosophical, psychological, and ethical dimensions.

# Endnotes

1. *American Literary Magazines: the Eighteenth and Nineteenth Centuries*, Edward E. Chielens, editor (New York: Greenwood, 1986), 364–69.
2. John E. Caswell, *Arctic Frontiers: United States Explorations in the Far North* (Norman: Univ. of Okla. Press, 1956), 68–88.
3. Robert Underwood Johnson to John Muir, December 12, 1894, *The John Muir Papers, 1858–1957*. Microform Edition. Ronald H. Limbaugh and Kirsten Lewis, eds. (Alexandria, VA: Chadwyck-Healey, Inc., 1986), 8/04687, hereafter JMP (microfilm).
4. John Muir to RU Johnson, October 10, 1894, JMP (microfilm) 8/04637.
5. Herbert L. Sussman, *Victorians and the Machine: the Literary Response to Technology* (Cambridge, Mass.: Harvard Univ. Press, 1968), 4–7.
6. Nina Baym, *Novels, Readers and Reviewers: Responses to Fiction in Antebellum America* (Ithaca and London: Cornell Univ. Press, c1984), 88.
7. John R. Reed, *Victorian Conventions* (Ohio Univ. Press, c1975), 132, 292.

8. John Muir diary [Ranch life], February 2, 1895, JMP (microfilm), 28/03226.

9. John Muir diary, February 12, 1895, JMP (microfilm), 28/03227.

10. John Muir diary, February 22, 1895, JMP (microfilm), 28/03230. The tentative title "Adventures on the Muir Glacier" suggests Muir now conceived of a single dog story with "Adventures" in the title. Earlier he appeared to suggest writing two stories, one about the dog and another covering other "adventures." But his letter to Johnson on February 23 clearly combined the two terms: "I shall now tackle the dog & the adventure." Muir to RU Johnson, JMP (microfilm), 8/04828. Muir was shocked when Johnson altered Muir's proposed title for the dog story, but the idea for the change may have stemmed from this early switch.

11. John Muir, Alaska Notes Summer of 1880 [ca. January 1895], unpublished manuscript notebook 00083, JMP (microfilm), 32/00123. This 98-page draft was one of Muir's first efforts to write an Alaska travel narrative. In this version he combined his 1880 and 1890 journal notes.

12. Ibid., 32/01120, p. 63.

13. Ibid., 32/01120, p. 64.

14. Jack London, for example, used his 15,000-volume library extensively for background and research, but only a fraction have been found to contain marginalia or notes. James Joyce wrote very few booknotes but developed a complicated system of dots found in at least 125 of some 700 titles identified as part of his personal library. From them Thomas J. Kenny discovered important clues to the origins of many words, passages and ideas in *Ulysses* and *Finnegan's Wake*. After studying marginal markings and brief notes in over 900 volumes from the private library of Eugene O'Neill, Kathy L. Bernard concluded that the American playwright used his books for overall inspiration as well as for historical accuracy. Even his best-known autobiographical plays such as *The Iceman Cometh* and *A Long Day's Journey into Night* contain philosophical as well as technical ideas that can be traced to specific volumes in O'Neill's personal library. Mary L. Ference, working almost entirely with secondary references, noted the philosophical and literary similarity between the works of Robert and Elizabeth Barret Browning and many of the authors of books they collected. Yet only a few of the 1700 items she identified from sales catalogs, research library descriptive guides, and other sources

contained significant holographic material. None of these collections has the wealth of notes, commentary, and draft text found in Muir's personal library. David M. Hamilton, *"The Tools of My Trade": Annotated Books in Jack London's Library* (Seattle & London: Univ. of Washington Press, 1986); Thomas J. Kenny, "His Plagiarist Pen: James Joyce's Marginal Markings in the Books of His Personal Library," (Ph.D. dissertation, New York University, 1975); Kathy L. Bernard, "The Research Library of Eugene O'Neill" (Ph.D. dissertation, Univ. of Mass., 1977); Mary L. Ference, The Library of Robert and Elizabeth Barrett Browning: A Preliminary Study (Unpublished Ph.D. dissertation, Univ. of Maryland, 1978).

15. Frederick Turner, *Rediscovering America: John Muir in His Time and Ours* (New York: Viking Penguin, 1985), 290–92.

16. Even Muir himself never resorted to this practice in composing any of his other books or articles, at least to the degree he did with the "Stickeen" text, although he did use the backs of books to work on some draft sentences and phrases for several writing projects he never completed. See holograph notes coded "Aurora," "Auto[biography]," and "Al[aska]" in the backs of books by John Brown, Thomas Carlyle, George Eliot, Hawthorne, Walter Scott, Ian Maclaren, and John Richard Green, and in other volumes in Muir's personal library, in the Holt-Atherton Library, University of the Pacific, hereafter cited as JML UOPWA.

17. See the appendix for an annotated listing.

18. S. Hall Young, *Alaska Days with John Muir* (New York: Fleming H. Revell, 1915), 188.

19. John Brown, *Rab and His Friends, and Other Papers and Essays* (London: J. M. Dent, [1907]), 7, 10.

20. John Brown, *Horae Subsecivae*. New edition in 3 vols. 2nd Series (Edinburgh: David Douglas, 1889). In John Muir Library, Holt-Atherton Library, University of the Pacific, hereafter JML UOPWA. All three volumes contain Keith's signature and date, 1891. In volume one, after Keith's name is the holograph inscription: "John Muir Martinez 92."

21. AMS notebook [untitled, 1896], p. 25, in JMP (microfilm), 33/01343.

22. Muir endnotes in Brown, *Horae Subsecivae,* vs. 1 & 2, in JML UOPWA.

23. For Carlyle's moral philosophy, see Charles F. Harrold, *Carlyle and German Thought, 1819–1834* (Hamdon & London: Archon Books, 1963), 2–29; Hippolyte A Taine, *History of English Literature,*

II(Brooklyn: Library Publishing Co., n.d.), 558–606; Robert Weisbuch, *Atlantic Double-cross: American Literature and British Influence in the Age of Emerson* (Chicago: Univ. of Chicago Press, 1986), 192–236; Linden Peach, *British Influence on the Birth of American Literature* (London: MacMillan, 1982), 78–83. For Muir's religious views see R. H. Limbaugh, "The Nature of Muir's Religion," *Pacific Historian*, 29 (Summer/Fall, 1985), 16–29.

24. Thomas Carlyle, *Critical and Miscellaneous Essays: Collected and Republished* (London: Chapman & Hall [1869?]), vol. 1, 321, JML UOPWA. The last line of the passage is an adaptation from the soliloquy in Act III of *Hamlet*, which neither Carlyle nor Muir bothered to acknowledge, though both were well versed in Shakespeare.

25. Hugh Miller, *The Life and Letters of Hugh Miller.* Edited by Peter Bayne, II (Boston Gould & Lincoln, 1871), 448, in JML UOPWA. Sometime after completing the "Stickeen" article, Muir purchased a twelve-volume edition of Miller's works, including Bayne's two-volume *Life and Letters*. The holograph endnotes demonstrate Muir's enduring interest in Miller: they cover much the same material, including the dog story that had attracted him earlier.

26. Carlyle, *Critical and Miscellaneous Essays*, vol. 2, 20, endnote, JML UOPWA.

27. John Muir holographic note in Carlyle, *History of Friedrich II of Prussia*, VI (London: Chapman & Hall [ca. 1870]), in JML UOPWA. Following the Stickeen notes is a sequence of page references and topical notes, proof that Muir read the book thoroughly after working on the dog story.

28. Muir endnote in Sir Walter Scott, *The Fortunes of Nigel.* Volume 8 of *Waverley Novels* (New York: George Routledge & Sons [1876?]), in John Muir Collection, Huntington Library, hereafter JMC HL.

29. Muir holographic notes in Nathaniel Hawthorne, *The Scarlet Letter* (Boston: Houghton Mifflin, 1884), in JML UOPWA.

30. Leo Marx, *The Machine in the Garden: Technology and the Pastoral Ideal in America* (New York: Oxford Univ. Press, 1967), 248; Carolyn Merchant, *The Death of Nature: Women, Ecology and the Scientific Revolution* (New York: Harper & Row, 1980, 1983), 225–28.

31. *My First Summer in the Sierra* (Boston and New York: Houghton Mifflin Co., 1911), 250.

32. Baym, *Novels, Readers and Reviewers*, 94–96.

33. Sir Walter Scott, *Fair Maid of Perth* (New York: George Routledge & Sons [1876?]), 236 and endnotes, in JMC HL.

34. Walter Scott, *The Blithedale Romance* (Boston: Houghton Mifflin, 1884), in JML UOPWA.

35. See chapter four, pages 68–69.

36. Nathaniel Hawthorne, *Our Old Home, and English Note-Books*, vol. 1 (Boston: Houghton Mifflin, 1884), 34, endnotes, in JML UOPWA.

37. John Muir diary, April 2, 1895, JMP (microfilm), 28/03238.

38. Ibid., April 8, 1895, JMP (microfilm), 28/03239.

39. Ibid., April 9. Sometime late in life Muir consoled a young author struggling to complete a dog story of his own. "Don't be in a hurry," said Muir, "it took me thirty years before I could get Stickeen across that narrow ice bridge." *Charles Kellogg, the Nature Singer, His Book* (1929), cited in William F. and Maymie B. Kimes, *John Muir: a Reading Bibliography* (Fresno, Calif.: Panorama West Books, 1986), 156.

40. John Muir diary, JMP (microfilm), 28/03243.

41. John Muir diary, May–June, 1895, JMP (microfilm), 28/03246–03258.

42. John Muir to RU Johnson, June 18, 1895, JMP (microfilm), 8/04928.

43. RU Johnson to John Muir, July 25, 1895, JMP (microfilm), 8/04949. Johnson said essentially the same thing in a letter the year before. RU Johnson to John Muir, May 17, 1894, JMP (microfilm), 8/04536.

44. John Muir diary, April 24, 1895, JMP (microfilm), 28/03249.

45. John Muir holograph note, ca. 1895, in JMP UOPWA, Series VI, "Related Articles & Scraps." Neither book was found in Muir's personal library at the University of the Pacific.

46. John Muir to Fay H. Sellers, November 11, 1895, 8/05043; John Muir to RU Johnson, February 27, 1896, 9/05129, both in JMP (microfilm).

47. Muir made no effort to identify the books from which his notes were taken, but a comparison of the endnotes and notebook entries makes clear that he transcribed notes from the following books in the sequence listed. Renan, *The Future of Science*; Eliot, *Wit and Wisdom*; Taine, *History of English Literature*; Goethe, *Wilhelm Meister's Apprenticeship*, v. 2; Hawthorne, *Our Old Home*, v. 1; Brown, *Horae Subsecivae*, v. 2; ibid., v. 1; Bagehot, *Literary Studies*, v. 1; Coleridge, *Table Talk*; Ruskin, *Modern Painters*, v. 1; Hawthorne, *Scarlet Letter*; *Mosses from an Old Manse*, v. 1; *The Blithedale Romance*; Ruskin, *Modern Painters*, v. 2; Scott, *Anne of Geierstein*; *Ivanhoe*; *Peveril of the Peak*; *Count Robert of Paris*; *The Fortunes of Nigel*; *The Heart of*

*Mid-Lothian*; Carlyle, *History of Friedrich II*, v. 2; Coleridge, *Poetical Works*, v. 1; Herbert, *Works;* Carlyle, *Oliver Cromwell's Letters and Speeches*, v. 5; *Tales by Musaeus; Critical and Miscellaneous Essays*, vs. 1–2.4; *The Life of John Sterling; History of Friedrich II*, v. 7; Scott, *The Pirate*; Parkman, *Pioneers of New France; Count Frontenac;* Plutarch, *Lives.*

48. C. Hart Merriam, "To the Memory of John Muir," *Sierra Club Bulletin*, 10 (Jan. 1917), 150.

49. John Muir diary, February 12, 1896, 28/03383; John Muir to RU Johnson, February 2, 1896, 9/05129; RU Johnson to John Muir, March 3, 1896, 9/05131, all in JMP (microfilm).

50. Muir journal entry, April 24, 1896, in JMP (microfilm) 28/03395.

51. "The National Parks and Forest Reservations," *Harper's Weekly* 41 (June 5, 1897): 563–67; "The American Forests," *The Atlantic Monthly* 80 (August 1897): 145–57.

52. John Muir to RU Johnson, October 28, 1896, JMP (microfilm), 9/05323.

53. S. H. Young to Muir, January 26, 1897, in JMP (microfilm) 9/05418.

54. S. Hall Young, The Veritable History of Stickine, unpublished manuscript [1897], JMP (microfilm), 51/00256. Young had returned to the states by the 1890s and was teaching in Ohio when Muir's letters reached him. He was overjoyed to hear from his old friend and granted Muir full rights to the dog reminiscence. Muir sent him a large check after learning that he was burdened with debt. SH Young to J Muir, January 26, February 9, 1897, JMP (microfilm), 9/05418, 05441.

55. S. Hall Young to John Muir, January 26, 1897, JMP (microfilm), 9/05418.

56. Charles W. Hawley, "Swedenborgianism on the Frontier," *Church History* VI (September 1937): 203–211.

57. Brother Cornelius, *Keith: Old Master of California*, I (New York: G. P. Putnam's Sons, 1942), 110.

58. Sampson Reed, *Observations on the Growth of the Mind,* 7th ed. (Chicago: E. B. Myers and Chandler, 1867), inscribed to Muir by Emerson; *Extracts from the Theological Works of Emanuel Swedenborg* (Boston: T. H. Carter, 1888); James J. G. Wilkinson, *Emanuel Swedenborg: A Biographical Sketch*, 2nd ed. (London: James Speirs, 1886); all JML UOPWA.

59. In "Mysterious Things" Muir recounts at least three instances in which he experienced psychic phenomena similar to Swedenborg's. Unpublished autobiography, ca. 1908, JMP (microfilm), 45/11517.

60. Brown, *Horae Subsecivae,* 1st series, JML UOPWA; John Muir notebook [Stickeen, etc.], p. 34, JMP (microfilm), 33/01347; John Muir notebook [Stickeen], p. 22, JMP (microfilm), 33/01410.

61. Linnie Marsh Wolfe reprinted the "herald" quotation in *John of the Mountains,* but did not trace its origins to the endnote in *Horae Subsecivae.*

62. Hawthorne, *The Marble Faun, or the Romance of Monte Beni,* vol. 1 (Boston: Houghton Mifflin, 1884), 221, endnote, in JML UOPWA.

63. *Stickeen,* 73–74.

64. *Critical and Miscellaneous Essays: Collected and Republished,* Vol. 3, p. 125, JML UOPWA.

65. John Muir, [Stickeen notebook], JMP (microfilm), 33/01345.

66. *The Listener in the Country* (Boston: Copeland & Day, 1896), 31–34, JML UOPWA.

67. Stickeen manuscript [1896], JMP (microfilm), 33/01351.

68. Ibid., 33/01379.

# Four

# "Stickeen" and the Lessons of Nature[1]

**M**uir's effort to enlarge the meaning of the "Stickeen" story was born of his revulsion against the anthropocentric arrogance he had witnessed as a youth. In his reminiscences he recalled incidents he later came to regret: letting a snapping turtle bite his dog's ear, throwing stones at a tomcat and dropping him from the roof, shooting birds, and robbing birds' nests.[2] On the Wisconsin farm as a young man he saw acts of wanton cruelty and ignorance that repelled him: farmers slaughtering songbirds by the hundreds to cash in on the local bounty, his father working a horse to death and killing the pet dog after he raided the chicken coop.[3] By 1867, on Muir's thousand-mile walk—a psychological journey as much as a physical trek through the American Southeast—he had developed a deep and abiding concern for the welfare of all creatures, sentient or simply alive.

That Muir's sympathy for animals was exceptional in an age of indifference is confirmed by numerous examples from his journals, correspondence, and publications. In *My First Summer* he condemned the "sport" of "seeking pleasure in the pain of fishes struggling for their lives," but in this instance he seemed more concerned with the desecration of Yosemite than the plight of the fish.[4] In *Travels in Alaska* he scolded Hunter Joe for shooting a seagull, an act the Indian said he had learned from whites who were "careless about taking life."[5] Gifford Pinchot, camping with Muir at Grand Canyon, noted with astonishment his refusal to allow a spider to be killed, and recorded his justification: "He said it had as much right there as we did."[6]

These are all familiar incidents to Muir scholars, but not so well known is the fact that most of Muir's unconventional animal views remained unknown during his active years as a wilderness writer and popularizer. As Lisa Mighetto has observed, Victorian readers "would not have approved of Muir's position."[7] Thus, even while privately condemning the wanton cruelty of "Lord Man," in public he mirrored the sentiment of his readers. There was little choice: publishers would not take risks. In his newspaper account of "Shasta game," for instance, he managed only to express a vague sympathy for the prey, but only after getting his blood up himself during the chase.[8] Even in his 1875 essay on "Wild Wool," his first published statement opposing the dominant view of the "world as made especially for the uses of man," he could not bring himself to criticize animal exploitation even while describing it. He ended the essay offering to help capture wild sheep in order to establish a more virile domestic breeding stock.[9]

Only in the last five years of his life did his editors begin to unveil a more outspoken Muir, and even then the exposure was tentative and cautious. The *A Thousand-Mile Walk to the Gulf* journal of 1867–1868, including Muir's famed condemnation of "Lord Man" for his arrogant presumption of moral superiority over the rest of creation, was not published until 1916. His defense of predators did not get a wide public hearing until the mid-1980s, when the Sierra Club published a collection of his writings, some for the first time.[10]

We are thus confronted with two discrete and somewhat incongruous images of John Muir, like two paintings by the same artist in different media and years apart. The contemporary image, made popular by books and articles published in his lifetime, reveals a naturalist with evocative descriptive powers, a metaphoric master craftsman, a nature advocate with a dynamic but overtly conventional message. The modern image is more radical. First formulated in the 1960s, it gave Muir an ecological cachet. New generations of scholars and activists rediscovered and reinterpreted his most provocative writings. At its crest in the 1970s, the green movement claimed him as one of their own, a radical activist, an iconoclast fighting to change the system. In 1972, one scholar, seeing a direct linkage between Muir's time and ours, credited him with "forecast[ing] the viewpoints, values and arguments of today's environmentalists and ecologists."[11]

Whether these contrasting images are accurate or even reconcilable is not within the scope of this book. But it is important to recognize that both competing impressions derive from the corpus of Muir's written work, published and unpublished. Like biblical exegesis, textual analysis of Muir's writings has often produced widely divergent interpretations.

Muir himself recognized the discrepancies between his public and private views, but his standard practice was to refuse to discuss matters of religion and family, or other subjects he considered too personal. Like Darwin, he did not want to hurt his family by openly attacking widely held beliefs. It was also not good business for a professional writer whose income, at least before the mid-1880s, depended to a large extent on reader interest. He therefore kept most of his thoughts to himself.[12]

But "Stickeen" was another matter. Producing a story with such inherent popular appeal opened a new window of opportunity. His lifework to the mid-nineties had concentrated on understanding and promoting nature and on encouraging mass appreciation of nature's beauty and diversity. He had previously written about animals, but mostly in uncontroversial terms that described but did not interpret. Now was his chance to teach as well as describe. Stickeen was more than just a clever dog; he was a messenger, a harbinger of good news about the natural world.

It was a timely message. The story of "Stickeen" emerged out of the intellectual foment of the 1890s, a disruptive decade of panic and depression, industrial exploitation and unparalleled labor violence, class consciousness and racism, imperialism and war. Accompanying these unsettling economic and social forces were profoundly disturbing scientific and intellectual challenges. After a generation of controversy, Darwinism still headed the list.[13] Thoughtful Americans at the turn of the century generally accepted the evidence of evolution but were deeply divided over its implications. Man and animal were closely related, but was the relationship good or bad?

Pessimists portrayed a dim future. To them Darwinism meant a literal descent of man to the level of animals, a Hobbesian confirmation that underneath the ethical facade were baser instincts that controlled human behavior. They lamented the loss of divinity, the moral as well as physiological diminution of the human species. Humans now had little to look forward to but the bleak struggle for existence like their cousin the brute. Novelists explored the dark side of human nature in fantasies such as *Dr. Jekyll and Mr. Hyde* and in realistic novels like *McTeague* and *Maggie, A Girl of the Streets*. Henry Adams summed up the somber implications: "In plain words, Chaos was the law of nature; Order was the dream of man."[14]

Optimists, in contrast, found ways to cushion society from such negative forebodings. One way was to tone down the materialist implications of Darwinism. Even Darwin himself was unwilling to reject theism openly.[15] Perhaps the human spirit, if not the human body, still contained the divine spark, the promise of dignity and nobility and progress.

A lifelong student and admirer of Darwin, Muir saw only the bright side. To him the ennobling qualities of life in man and the higher animals confirmed the divine spark. Beauty and harmony in the physical world were patent evidence of a benevolent and loving creator. Instead of demonstrating "might makes right," evolution was purposive, ongoing and progressive, all part of the divine plan.[16]

Darwinians also countered the negativists by elevating the moral status of animals. Using animals to teach moral truths is nothing new in literature. The practice dates at least to the sixth century B.C., when Aesop provided moral instruction through tales that endowed "beasts with the attributes of human beings."[17] As philosopher Albert Borgmann has recently observed, western culture has constantly struggled with the meaning of nature, often failing to distinguish between the real and the artificial in seeking to learn its lessons. Even domestic dogs, an artificial construct literally created by humans through selective breeding practices, "can speak to us in meaningful ways."[18]

Nature writing in the 1890s expanded upon a premise explored a half-century earlier by Romantic primitivists: nature was a source of moral truth, free from the corrupting influences of ignoble humanity. To progressive Americans, raw nature was less appealing than pastoral nature, tamed and modified by the hand of man while still embodying primal virtues.[19] Even the family pet had admirable mental and moral qualities. The result was a new literary genre, the noble animal story.[20]

Thus, in Muir's notes, Stickeen emerged reborn, a dog with deeper and more enduring elements of character than anyone, even Muir, had observed in life or described by word of mouth. The new Stickeen required some remodeling and a certain amount of poetic license. But during the 1890s, when Americans began a process of reinventing nature that still continues a century later,[21] Muir was convinced the dog story could be shaped into a powerful didactic instrument, a tool to help Americans understand and appreciate their fellow creatures.

Stickeen's moral worth rested not on the logic of Darwinian materialism but on Muir's belief that all living things are linked by a chain of creation. The Great Chain of Being, adapted from Greek ontology by Christian theologians to explain the origin and organization of life in the universe, influenced western thought for more than a thousand years. Extolled by medieval scientists, philosophers, and poets alike, it postulated a coherent and preordained hierarchy of creatures beginning with the lowest and ascending in orderly steps to the ultimate creator-god. Sixteenth-century Italian philosopher Giordano Bruno expressed a version Muir rated "all g[ood] and more" because of its implications for evolution and animal equality. "The mind of man," said Bruno, "differs from that of lower animals and of plants not in quality but only in quantity. . . . Each individual is the resultant of innumerable individuals. Each species is the starting point for the next. . . . No individual is the same to-day as yesterday."[22]

The chain of being theory and its variants slowly disintegrated after 1600 as empirical science exposed the fallacy of a priori assumptions about the natural world, a process Carolyn Merchant has characterized as the "death of nature."[23] The theory might have died peacefully had it not been for the Romantics. They gave it new life by disputing the Enlightenment model of a mechanistic universe, static and immutable. Instead, Romantics emphasized individuality. They conceived of an organismic model, a boundless and dynamic process of creativity that found underlying unity in diversity—thus opening the door to evolutionary thinking without utterly destroying the religious premise on which the great-chain theory was based. In the United States Emerson led the way, building upon ideas from Coleridge, Wordsworth, and Carlyle. The Sage of Concord asserted in "Correspondences" that

the universe is represented in every one of its particles. Everything in nature contains all the powers of nature. Everything is made of one hidden stuff; as the naturalist sees one type under every metamorphosis, and regards a horse as a running man, a fish as a swimming man, a bird as a flying man, a tree as a rooted man. Each new form repeats not only the main character of the type, but part for part all the details, all the aims, furtherances, hindrances, energies, and whole system of every other.[24]

Post-Darwinian creation-scientists like Asa Gray, Alfred Russell Wallace, and John Muir had little trouble reconciling empirical biology with belief in a purposive and harmonious universe.[25] As James Rachels has pointed out, Darwinism and creationism are not necessarily incompatible.[26] Even Darwin's own personal agnosticism, had it been known publicly, might have made little difference to theists. Muir noted with approval a passage from Darwin's *Beagle* journal, speculating that a systematic study of ovenbirds in Bahia Blanca "ultimately may assist in revealing the grand scheme, common to the present and past ages, on which organized beings have been created."[27] All life was still linked and unified by a cosmic chain, created and maintained by a divine master planner.[28]

Through the books of his personal library Muir absorbed ideas from Romantic defenders of the chain of being theory, including Goldsmith, Kant, Herder, Schiller, Swedenborg, Coleridge, Emerson, Thoreau, and Carlyle. Holographic notes and marginalia show how important such views were to the development of Muir's own thinking. From Emerson's words quoted above, Muir formulated his own anthropocentric theory of oneness, insisting, like Emerson, that "all of Nature is found in man. Squeeze all the universe into the size & shape of a perfect human soul & that is a whole man."[29] In the back of a volume of Asa Gray's scientific papers, Muir noted the Harvard botanist's affirmation of the "Infinite Variety in Unity wh[ich] characterizes the Creators works."[30] In Carlyle's *Life of John Sterling* Muir underscored Sterling's reference to the "sense of a oneness of life and power in all existence," but rephrased it to the "sense of a oneness of life & destiny in all existence."[31] An original aphorism Muir pencilled in Wallace's metaphysical treatise *The World of Life* expresses even more directly the influence of chain theory on the California Scot: "Every cell, every particle of matter in O [the world] requires a Captain to steer it into its place JM"[32] Finally, in the midst of a lengthy series of notes on "Stickeen" written on the endpages of Hawthorne's *The Scarlet Letter*, Muir tried to draft a more explicit statement on oneness:

> Like a voice from the upper heights came the message you & I are one/ Through so humble a medium came the apostolic message dog & man[,] all animals/ & man are one/ Looking into the eyes/ watching the attitudes of snakes bedbugs etc I felt dimly that no line of demarcation separated us.[33]

Here Muir's creator imagery blurred the distinctions between species and asserted an egalitarian view of life in the cosmos. Peel back superficial differences and life forms become indistinguishable, either by the nature of their essences or by their moral worth. This was the central message Muir found in reassessing the meaning of Stickeen. The logic of the Great Chain of Being led him to a reaffirmation of the moral equality of dogs and men and all other elements in the endless span of creation. In an advanced draft of the "Stickeen" manuscript he reinforced the point in a mystical acknowledgment of Stickeen's role as heavenly messenger. "The vast mysterious chain of being," he wrote, taking the line straight from Coleridge,[34] "about as little known as are the inhabitants of other stars. That they should in such lively demonstrative multitudes be with us & remain so strangely apart from us is most wonderful."[35]

Stickeen was thus a special dog, an individual personality with inherent worth. Muir's nature writing, flowing from what has been called the "humanitarian" branch of the conservation movement, asserted the individuality of animals both as a way to uplift their moral value in the eyes of the reading public and as a ploy against utilitarian conservationists, who sought scientific studies of aggregate animal populations and who tended to treat animals as objects to be managed like forests and grasslands.[36] The humanitarians deplored the depersonalization of species and emphasized individual personality characteristics. "It is the denial of 'personality' to animals that is at the root of the evil," wrote Henry Salt, one of the most outspoken and well-known humanitarians.[37] By appealing to reader sympathies, humanitarians helped expand popular interest in the cause of animal rights. Yet by describing individual animal characteristics in anthropomorphic terms, many popular writers enveloped nature with a Romantic gloss.[38]

In his study of nature, Muir stood somewhere between the scientific method and unadulterated anthropomorphism. By describing Stickeen's personality traits, he sought to make his canine nature and actions understandable to the ordinary reader of popular magazines. He knew that what his readers wanted was not, as a contemporary literary critic put it, a "faithful representation of animals as they actually are," but animal characterization emphasizing the "matters and customs of men." This "human note" would provide "didactic and moral" lessons that would ensure the enduring place of animal literature in popular imagination.[39] Muir probably thought that was what Gerald Griffin, an early nineteenth-century Irish poet and novelist, had in mind when he described a dog closing the door behind his master while a stupefied onlooker exclaimed: "Well . . . that flogs cock-fighting! I never thought I'd live to have a dog taich me manners, anyway. . . ."[40]

Muir's friend John Burroughs also recognized the need to observe and describe animals in human terms but warned against trying to make more out of animal behavior than the facts warranted. He scornfully rejected the anthropomorphic characterizations of most Romantic nature writers, but praised Muir's dog story for elucidating animal character without stretching credulity. "It is true that Muir makes his dog act like a human being under the press of great danger," he wrote, "but the action is not the kind that involves reason; it only implies sense perception, and the instinct of self-preservation. Stickeen does as his master bids him, and he is human only in the human emotions of fear, despair, joy that he shows."[41]

But Burroughs did not know the original Stickeen, the dog Muir described in the first complete written version that his editor gutted. That version implied the dog had more than mere "sense perception."

Burroughs, Muir, and other contemporary naturalists drew conclusions about animals based on field observations of individual specimens, but they leaned toward evidence that was anecdotal rather than empirically testable. Sustained field observation, rather than laboratory testing, was the approved method of nature study in late nineteenth century.[42] The old ways died hard, as John Burroughs demonstrated in criticizing lab tests. Tests "prove what the animal does not know and cannot do under artificial conditions, but do they show what it does know and can do under natural conditions?"[43] Muir would have thought it a fair question. He was no specialist on dogs, but after nearly a month of togetherness in the field he believed he knew Stickeen thoroughly.

Muir's moral egalitarianism drew him closer to activists in the cause of animal rights. Like so many other modernist trends near the turn of the century, the late Victorian movement for animal rights grew out of the foment over the intellectual and moral implications of natural selection. Before Darwin, Christian thought about animals had been dominated by dogmas arising from the creation story in Genesis and from classical Greek philosophy, both proclaiming human moral superiority. Adam's obligation to "multiply and subdue the earth" had perhaps more dynamic impact on growth and development in the western world than Plato's more subtle influence. Yet Plato not only exalted humans as the only creatures with souls, he also gave them a loftier material status. They were, in effect, gods in an animal body. While disputing Plato's taxonomy, Aristotle also elevated humans by defining them as the highest order in the animal kingdom. He endowed both humans and animals with souls but distinguished between the immortal soul of the human species and the material soul of animals that died with the body. Thus for much of western history, religion and philosophy both reinforced the notion of human dominion and moral superiority. Animals had no special status on earth, no place in the hereafter, and no moral worth.[44]

Moral and biological superiority, however, did not justify mistreatment. Medieval Christian stewardship doctrine, exemplified by the teachings of St. Francis, the patron saint of some modern environmentalists,[45] condemned wanton cruelty.[46] Regardless of whether they had souls, the higher animals, at least, felt pain, and to expose any creature deliberately to needless suffering was considered an egregious sin. This traditional Christian sympathy for animals gave way during the eighteenth century Enlightenment to the mechanistic rationalism of René Descartes, who reduced all but human life to the status of dumb animals or plants. Even though both animals and man were machines, he wrote, only humans had souls and only souls were sentient. Animals were thus "incapable of feeling."[47]

By asserting the primacy of human over all other life forms, Cartesian dualism reinforced the idea of human progress at the expense of less worthy objects. From Descartes to Darwin and beyond, the industrial revolution swept across the western world, sanctified by an anthropocentric philosophy and armed with new technology that accelerated nature's conquest and domination. In this 200-year era, romanticism was the only major intellectual movement to challenge the logic of exploitation, but much of its psychic energy was siphoned off in sentimental appeals on behalf of life's downtrodden, including slaves, orphans, aborigines, imbeciles, women, and "dumb" animals.

In the meantime, as early as the eighteenth century, Cartesian dualism came under increasing pressure from moral philosophers and materialists. John Locke, David Hartley, and Étienne de Condillac, forerunners of modern animal psychology, did not reject dualism but recognized "continuous degrees of intelligence at various levels of the scale of beings."[48] De la Mettrie's sensational *L'Homme machine* (1748) proposed a wholly mechanistic view of the chain of being. "If one [animal] has soul, so has the other; if one is a machine so is the other." He would have converted psychology to a study of physiology.[49] Up to the mid-nineteenth century the emerging disciplines of psychology and biology struggled to reconcile the idea of a continuous material chain with older notions that separated mind from matter.

Then came Darwin and the revolutionary implications of natural selection. The *Origin of the Species* (1859) was a watershed in the transition from Romantic to Victorian science.[50] By the 1890s Darwinism had clouded both Cartesian and Romantic views of the animal-human relationship. In trumpeting the common biology of animals and humans, radical Darwinians, as distinguished from post-Darwinian creationists, replaced transcendental metaphysics with materialism. Even if Darwin himself was reluctant to abandon creationism publicly, his German apostle Ernst Haeckel was much bolder. He antagonized both Neoplatonists and orthodox Christians by insisting that all higher brain functions, like all motor functions, evolved from lower organisms.[51] Despite the resistance of theists like Muir, the implications of Haeckel's uncompromising materialism extended the debate over the causes of animal behavior as well as the moral status of animals.

The holographic marks and marginalia in books Muir read during this era demonstrate how closely he followed these debates and illustrate his effort to expand his dog story into a larger study of animal behavior and its lessons for humanity. Darwinians in the late Victorian era raised three troubling issues of special interest to Muir: the ethical relationship between humans and animals, the nature and extent of animal intelligence, and the status of the soul in higher animals. Of less direct impact on his manuscript, but still influential in shaping Muir's thinking during the long gestation of "Stickeen," was a fourth question that grew out of the debates on the other three: did all sentient beings, including women, have fundamental rights men were bound to respect?

By insisting that sentience, along with ganglia and the central cortex, was a product of natural selection common to all higher animals, strident evolutionists cast a shadow over traditional ethics which had hitherto ignored or discounted nonhuman species. If making others suffer is unethical, any being that can experience pain deserves respect and consideration. Jeremy Bentham had first postulated this principle in the late eighteenth century, and it was taken up in earnest in the renewed debates of the 1890s.[52]

The question of sentience led to a renewed dispute over the question of animal intelligence. Muir flatly rejected the view of some contemporary animal psychologists that instinct was at the root of animal behavior. Frederick W. Badé recalled a Berkeley gathering, probably in 1909, when Muir and Burroughs argued over the issue. Muir's point of view "in the judgment of those present scored heavily against his opponent."[53] The debate was not recorded, but in Muir's 1897 notes on "Stickeen" we have a good example of what he might have said:

[I]n our ignorance & pride how calmly & lazily we slump the whole question of our relationship [with animals] into the blurred fetish word "Instinct" a word that contains more lazy selfish arrogant ignorance than anything in human language . . . This one fetish word thus allowing the languid inquiries to enjoy the comfort & confidence of a superior sort of ignorance branded 'Science'[54]

Muir's belief in the cognition of sentient creatures found common ground with Ernst Haeckel and other Darwinians who rejected Cartesian logic along with Romantic sentiment. Romantics and Cartesians alike had assumed animal behavior was motivated solely by instinct. But if humans and animals have similar nervous systems and brain functions, why should reasoning ability be exclusively human? Darwin and his bulldog of an advocate, Thomas Huxley, found it difficult to reject that logic.[55] They were reinforced by other post-Darwinians, including Nathaniel S. Shaler, a Harvard geologist. In *The Interpretation of Nature,* a book Muir read during the drafting of "Stickeen," Shaler asked what motivates animals to seek human sympathy and affection. "The only logical explanation," he said, answering his own question, "is found in the conclusion that the mind of the animal goes out to his master from the same sympathetic reason which leads the master to love him."[56]

Another scientist whose work Muir had read was George H. Romanes, a pioneer in the field of comparative psychology. Darwin had encouraged him to study animal behavior as a model for deciphering human evolution.[57] He also used "common sense" in attempting to understand why animals and humans may develop similar "mental states." In a passage Muir underscored, Romanes explained animal intelligence by a modernized version of chain theory:

Just as the theologians tell us—and logically enough—
that if there is a Divine Mind, the best, and indeed
only, conception we can form of it is that which is
formed on the analogy, however imperfect, supplied
by the human mind; so with 'inverted anthropomorphism' we must apply a similar consideration with a
similar conclusion to the animal mind.[58]

Romanes's study was filled with anecdotes describing animal behavior analogous to that of humans in species ranging from
insects to primates. It made a deep impression on Muir,[59] who
devoured the chapters on bees and dogs—both species he had
personally investigated. Although cautioning himself in an endnote
on a backpage of Romanes's book that "Analogies in nature studies
[are] apt to be misleading,"[60] he nevertheless found in the Romanes
tract reinforcement for his conviction that Stickeen's action on
the glacier was more than mere instinct. "The reasoning displayed
by dogs may not always be of a high order," wrote Romanes in a
passage Muir found of particular interest, "but little incidents,
from being of constant occurrence among all dogs, are the more
important as showing the reasoning facility to be general to these
animals."[61] Applying this conclusion to Stickeen, Muir wrote on
the back pages of Romanes's book:

Can we conceive any human being reasoning more
correctly under the desparate circumstances than
Stick[een]/ Not from a mere love of anecdote do I write
this but to throw light on the vast animal world/ The
fear of thoughts & feelings that I saw {under a stern
death & life press} in this lit[tle] d[og] cannot I think
fail to interest every human thinker/ Never as far as
I know had a d[og] ever before been confronted by
so stern & fateful a problem . . . all his movements

& gestures became fairly luminous with reason &
intelligence[62]

If animals could think like humans, did they also have fundamental rights? Victorian scientists had difficulty reconciling the
theory of evolution with issues of morality.[63] But the moral implications of Darwinism were not lost on a new coalition of animal
rights activists who emerged as the nineteenth century closed.
One of the most vocal, and widely read, was an English liberal,
Henry S. Salt, whose 1892 treatise summed up the new case for
animal rights. By setting humans apart from animals, by denying
animal immortality or sentience, said Salt, Christian dogma and
Cartesian epistemology share the blame for centuries of indifference and cruelty to animals. Now science had demonstrated that
animals and humans share a similar biological heritage. Extrapo-
lating from that premise, Salt concluded that animals have "individuality, character, reason; and to have those qualities is to have
the right to exercise them, insofar as surrounding circumstances
permit."[64]

Salt's impassioned plea called public attention to issues that
had been debated for years among intellectuals both in Europe
and the United States. Before Darwin, sympathy for dumb animals was the common denominator by which animal advocates
appealed for better treatment. Darwinism added a new twist by
strengthening the argument of activists who asserted that animals were intelligent as well as morally equivalent to humans.

A revolutionary affirmation, indeed, but conditioned by the
pragmatic realities of surrounding circumstances. Like other moral
reformers, animal rights activists had to overcome the inertia and
indifference of established traditions and institutions. Institutional
religion, the political system, the schools, mass opinion—all
resisted change. Animal rights sounded ominous to working
people, especially if they depended on animal exploitation for a

livelihood. Even Darwinism itself could be used to work against social intervention for any reason. By drawing dubious analogies between natural selection among species and survival of the fittest in human society, English philosopher Herbert Spencer transformed Social Darwinism into a justification for economic and social laissez-faire. Thus public indifference, even public hostility, greeted early advocates of animal rights. Before corrective action could be taken, the movement needed to gather allies, to build a broad base of sympathy and support.

Muir's extant library does not contain Salt's 1892 treatise, but the book may have been one of the 300 or so lost after 1914. That Muir and Salt knew the work of each other, however, is more than just surmise: the Muir papers contain correspondence from Salt after 1900, and one of Salt's later books, personally inscribed by the author and annotated by Muir in endnotes, resides in the Holt-Atherton Library. Muir shared Salt's view on the deleterious effects of Christian dogma, the damage done by Cartesian dualism, and the need to recognize and respect animal rights. But he went beyond Salt and most humanitarians in defending predators.[65] Twenty years before Salt's publication, Muir had proclaimed rights for all living things:

> Ours is an age [of] liberal principles yet we find but little charity that is broad enough to include bears. A Burns may step outside the selfish circle of his species with sympathy for a suffering daisy or to claim the mousie as fellow mortal but in the smug highwalled realms of the civilized such souls are rare indeed & it is boasted as a grand consummation of "universal charity" that now all the human race black brown & yellow are recognized as in some sence brethren capable of christianity & even admissible to the Anglo Saxon heaven, but bears are allowed no part nor loft in our

celestial regions & are begrudged the air & light. . . . all long toothed poisonous uneatable uncivilizable animals & plants wh carry prickles are vaguely considered diabolical or . . . in some way referrable to man's first disobedience. . . . Man forms but a small portion of the great unit of creation & bears & snakes have rights as well as he.[66]

Despite growing interest in protecting animals, the Victorian world was not ready for such revolutionary ethics. Most of Muir's writings in defense of predators remained in the closet during his lifetime, and even his literary executors were reluctant to reveal the real Muir.[67] Salt, however, had no such qualms. His 1892 publication, even though it stopped short of calling for predator rights, established his reputation as a leader of the animal rights movement.

By that time Muir was also famous but much less controversial. His popularity rested on carefully crafted published descriptions of the beautiful western wilds where he had wandered and preached the gospel of preservation. Thousands had read his eloquent prose in *Scribners, Harper's,* and *Century;* they knew him not as a revolutionary but as the spokesman for America's rich natural heritage. And they were willing listeners, if not ready converts, for the 1890s was an era of reflection, a time for soul-searching and reassessment. If the nation owed its greatness to the frontier, as historian Frederick Jackson Turner asserted, what would the future offer now that the frontier was but a memory? Muir's charming portraits of redwood giants, sublime vistas, and animal personalities tamed the Wild West with evocative word pictures. He was a popularizer, a spokesman for the picturesque, a naturalist with a national following. Both he and his editors recognized the power of his persuasive but gentle rhetoric. But there were also penalties for popularity. Writing for the masses placed boundaries on literary discretion. Johnson's editorial hand kept Muir confined to words, themes, and values to which the American people were already accustomed.

But Salt's work and the animal rights movement stirred Muir's conscience and rekindled the revolutionary fires that smoldered within. The momentum for change seemed to be leaning his way. Witness the string of recent conservation victories: the new park bills passed in 1890 for Yosemite and Sequoia, and the 1892 founding of the Sierra Club. If he could popularize conservation, perhaps he could do the same for animal rights. The trick was to challenge traditional attitudes in an inoffensive way, to reach the public's heart with a sentimental story that unobtrusively introduced radical concepts.

That was the formidable task that so complicated the writing of "Stickeen." Even demonstrating the dog's intelligence was made more difficult by Johnson's insistence on following literary conventions. To retain the element of surprise, the *Century* editor wanted Muir to introduce Stickeen as a "dull" dog with little hint of intellect until confronted by the great crevasse. For months the author struggled to find just the right phrasing. On the backpages of books, on tablets, and on scraps of paper he tried out various combinations: "Serenity seemed only dullness,"[68] "a dull sleepy sagacity,"[69] "dull glum feeble dignity,"[70] "the little dull dumbness of a dog,"[71] "a dull silly semi-imbecile look,"[72] and the more alliterative "small black dumpling of dullness."[73] After at least sixty different trial runs, he finally settled on six separate characterizations of the dog's evident dim-witted behavior in the final draft of 1897. Johnson cut those down to three in the published version.

But why was the dog so insensible? The primitivist in Muir initially claimed the dog was "dulled by civilization,"[74] yet, on second thought, nineteenth-century Alaska was hardly the place to stake that claim. But the other alternative, attributing dullness to mongrelism, was worse, for it contradicted his belief, expressed in "Wild Wool" and other essays, that "all wildness is finer than tameness."[75] Confronted by a dilemma, Muir compromised. By the final draft, he vaguely attributed Stickeen's dullness to the heritage of "generations of downtrodden ancestors" worn out by hard work and hunting.[76]

Muir's manuscript thus described the little dog on the wrong side of the glacial abyss as an unknown entity, a canine "of the dull solemn kind,"[77] ponderous and stoical, an unlikely object of human interest or concern. A dog with hidden intellectual powers, that was the message. To cross the crevasse, courage had to conquer fear, inspiration to triumph over instinct. But courage and inspiration were more than just discrete intellectual gifts. They were attributes of the soul, the "central drama of all Emerson's work,"[78] the organizing principle that gave meaning to much of mankind in the late Victorian era.[79] Darwinian materialism had undermined the metaphysical pedestal on which the soul rested, yet the defenders of tradition—novelists, essayists, even some scientists—fought back on both sides of the Atlantic.[80] Richard Jefferies, a popular English nature essayist well represented in Muir's library, resorted to negative evidence: "merely because after death the soul is not visible is no demonstration that it does not still live."[81] In the United States, popular journals like *Nineteenth Century* and *Atlantic Monthly* carried on a resurgent debate over the nature, existence, and immortality of the soul, a dialogue that reached its peak during Muir's writing of "Stickeen."

Defenders of tradition had to respond to two types of criticism. One came from positivists like Haeckel, who either insisted that all psychic processes follow the "law of substance," or like Thomas Huxley, who took refuge in Voltairian agnosticism. On immortality, for instance, Huxley said that "I see no reason for believing in it, but, on the other hand, I have no means of disproving it."[82] To "cultivate your own garden" meant avoiding irrelevant metaphysical questions.[83] The other type was less materialistic but equally disturbing, for it granted the existence of souls while heretically broadening the concept to include the higher nonhuman species. All things were related by a common substance, but did that include mind as well as matter? And did each level of life contain all the attributes of the soul? Emerson had reopened a metaphysical Pandora's Box by finding a common denominator in the "hidden stuff" with which all things are created.[84]

Other creationists also saw the logic of continuity, especially as Darwinism continued to chip away at theoretical distinctions between humans and other animals. If there were no differences in material substance, why should there be differences in spirit? The question did not worry Sydney Smith, English clergyman and critic. During an earlier controversy over evolution, he tried to soothe troubled waters with a dose of common sense: "I feel so sure that the blue ape without a tail [i.e., a baboon] will never rival us in poetry, painting, and music, that I see no reason whatever that justice may not be done to the few fragments of soul and tatters of understanding which they may really possess."[85] In the 1870s Thomas Huxley proffered an organic distinction: evolution explains consciousness, but higher brain functions may develop only at the higher stages of evolution. But lest religionists take comfort in believing animals "do not possess immortal souls," he admitted that his theory would not "prevent any one from entertaining the amiable convictions ascribed by Pope to his untutored savage, that, when he passed to the realms of the blessed, his faithful dog should bear him company."[86]

On the immortality of dog souls Muir stood four-square with the "savages." Scottish poet John Wilson voiced Muir's own inner thoughts: "I hae never been able to persuade my heart and my understandin' that dowgs haena immortal sowls."[87] A lifelong critic of sectarian dogmas, Muir rejected all arguments that smacked of speciesism, the assumption that one species is morally superior to another. Like Pope, he saw the irony in contrasting "primitive" and "civilized" religions. "Even in religion animals are mostly ignored," Muir scoffed. "We throw our heaven open to every vertical mammal but close it against all the horizontal ones. Indians are more charitable. They allow their dogs to follow them into their happy hunting grounds."[88] This was bold, indeed—too bold for his editor. Johnson deleted the passage. But he left the idea in Muir's closing line, which referred to immortality but offered it only as a quaint personal conviction, rather than an emphatic affirmation: "to me Stickeen is immortal."[89]

In his story, Muir also wanted to address the matter of animal souls. That the dog had a soul was to him beyond doubt, but like Scott, in speculating about the destiny of his favorite old bitch, he "dare not say soul!" without qualification, lest some readers protest.[90] The solution was to elevate the dog's soul to human status to make the idea more palatable to his readers. That led him to the idea of metempsychosis, or the transmigration of souls from humans to animals.

This was an old theory, traceable at least as far back as Pythagoras in the western world and ancient Hindu philosophy in the East.[91] The concept fostered belief in the immortality of souls and also laid the cornerstone for a broader ethic. In the West, faith in incarnate immortality, if not reincarnation, remained a fundamental tenet of Christianity long after transmigration theory declined. But the notion of metempsychosis resurfaced and gained considerable attention by the 1890s as part of the backwash of Darwinism.

Muir had entertained the transmigration theory as early as 1871, when he had read Emerson's affirmation of the idea.[92] As his endnote in Hawthorne's *Our Old Home* demonstrates, he considered using it to explain the phenomenon of Stickeen, who "Seemed to be conscious of the dawn of some wondrous good fortune. No wonder the belief is so widespread of transmigration of souls & everybody obsessed with psychological speculations as to whether they have souls." By 1896, Muir had worked that cumbersome passage down into a terse: "No wonder so many believe the souls of men enter animals."[93] In an advanced draft of 1897, after reading Thomas Browne's *Religio Medici,* Muir took a more precautionary tack. Browne, a seventeenth-century English physician whose essays explored the rocky ground between Enlightenment science and religious orthodoxy, had dismissed the transmigration theory as nonsense: "I cannot believe the wisdom of Pythagoras did ever positively, and in a literal sense, affirm his Metempsychosis, or impossible transmigration of the Souls of men into beasts."[94] Muir's revised draft reflected Browne's sobering assessment: "No wonder so many believe or half believe the Pythagorian notion {doctrine} of transmigration of souls."[95] That was essentially how it appeared in the final version, but Johnson deleted it before publishing the story in 1897.

As the story began to take final form, Muir thought of another way to explain the animal's special talents. He conceived the ice bridge as a metaphor for baring the soul. The moment of truth came in Stickeen's decision to cross the bridge. Here was the crisis that "like white light laid the mind and soul bare."[96] "Now his whole soul & body to the end of every hair was revealed."[97] What Muir conceived was a confirmation of oneness, a symbolic union of man and animal. For in beholding Stickeen's soul, Muir saw himself. Stickeen was a boy growing up, a wayward child suddenly transformed by crisis. The glacial journey was a metaphor for life, with Muir and the dog at the moment of crisis moving in concert, with mind and spirit fused together in a coalescence of the primal elements of creation. "Soul of our soul," wrote Muir. "Under the stress of this supreme trial Stickine became a living human soul."[98]

If the bridge was the connecting link between the species, the abyss symbolized the dark unknown, the void of superstition and fear that separates human from other life forms. Bridging the gap represented not only oneness and immortality—a uniting of souls in a spiritual victory over death—it also signified a "triumphant joy of deliverance"[99] from the netherworld of ignorance that prevented mankind from recognizing its physical and spiritual kinship with the rest of creation. Leaving the void behind was, to Muir, symbolic affirmation of the human-animal bond.

From its initial telling in the 1880s to the final version submitted in 1897, Muir's dog story, like Darwin's ovenbirds, changed over time. What began as an exotic personal adventure exploring a rugged glacial wilderness evolved into a lesson in the moral equality and oneness of all animate life. Incorporating concepts gleaned from nearly two decades of reading and reflection, Muir's final narrative contained unconventional ideas, some of which his editor found too sensitive to publish in a popular magazine in the waning Victorian years.[100] But the editor left intact the author's bedrock lessons, the culminating wisdom of his moral education. Outspoken defender of wilderness values, John Muir was also an eloquent spokesman for animals. Even if material evolution led to divergent paths, in his thinking all higher animals were endowed with the creator's gifts of intellect, sentience, and immortality. As proof he offered first-hand evidence gathered on a glacier in 1880 with a "little hank of hair" named Stickeen.

# Endnotes

1.  In earlier version of this chapter was published under the title "Stickeen and the Moral Education of John Muir," in *Environmental History Review* 15 (Spring 1991): 25–45.

2.  John Muir, *The Story of My Boyhood and Youth* (Boston and New York: Houghton Mifflin, 1913), 24–26, 47–48, 80, 149–58. In his early years in Yosemite he killed a rattlesnake but never did so again, even though he found one in his Yosemite cabin. See journal excerpts in *John of the Mountains: The Unpublished Journals of John Muir*. Edited by Linnie Marsh Wolfe (Boston: Houghton Mifflin, 1938; Madison: Univ. of Wisconsin Press, 1979), 28.

3.  Muir, *Boyhood and Youth*, 82–83, 107–10, 168–69.

4.  John Muir, *My First Summer in the Sierra* (Boston and New York: Houghton Mifflin, 1911), 255–56.

5.  John Muir, *Travels in Alaska* (Boston & New York: Houghton Mifflin, c1915), 235.

6.  Gifford Pinchot, *Breaking New Ground* (Seattle & London: Univ. of Washington Press, c1947, 1972), 103.

7.  Lisa Mighetto, *John Muir and the Rights of Animals*, xxii–iii. See also her article, "John Muir and the Rights of Animals," *Pacific Historian* 29 (Summer/Fall, 1985): 107–09. It should be noted that although Muir showed ecological insight in describing the importance of predators for balancing certain habitats, he is not regarded among the founders of the modern science of ecology.

8.  John Muir, "Shasta Game: Hunting the Wild Sheep and Mule Deer . . . ," San Francisco *Daily Evening Bulletin*, December 12, 1874, p. 8, c. 1. For an expanded version of the same episode see *John of the Mountains*, 193–200.

9.  John Muir, "Wild Wool," *Overland Monthly* (April 1875), reprinted in *John Muir Wilderness Essays* (Salt Lake City: Peregrine Smith, 1980), 227–42. Michael Cohen labels the essay as "probably the best ecological argument of his [Muir's] career," but notes that Muir refused to venture into a broad-scaled attack on animal exploitation. Cohen, *The Pathless Way: John Muir and American Wilderness* (Madison: Univ. of Wisconsin Press, 1984), 175–81.

10. *Muir Among the Animals*, edited by Lisa Mighetto (San Francisco: Sierra Club Books, c1986).

11. J. S. Holliday, "The Politics of John Muir," *Sierra Club Bulletin* 57 (October–November 1972): 10.

12. Roderick Nash has concluded that politics, not personal, family or commercial considerations, restrained Muir in public, although that does not explain his reluctance to speak out on certain issues long before he "got into politics and became pragmatic." Roderick F. Nash, *The Rights of Nature: A History of Environmental Ethics* (Madison: Univ. of Wisconsin Press, c1989), 41. I agree with the position taken earlier by Judson McGehee, that Muir's reticence was due more to "personal modesty." McGehee, "The Nature Essay as a Literary Genre: an Intrinsic Study of the Works of Six English and American Nature Writers" (Ph.D. dissertation, Univ. of Michigan, 1958), 62.

13. Roderick Nash, *Wilderness and the American Mind* 3rd ed. (New Haven and London: Yale Univ. Press, c1967, 1982), 143–45.

14. Lisa Mighetto, "Science, Sentiment and Anxiety: American Nature Writing at the Turn of the Century," *Pacific Historical Review* LIV

(February 1985): 33–34; James Turner, *Reckoning with the Beast: Animals, Pain, and Humanity in the Victorian Mind* (Baltimore & London: Johns Hopkins Univ. Press, c1980), 62, 67; Henry Adams, *The Education of Henry Adams* (Boston: Houghton Mifflin, c1918, 1961), 451.

15.  Before publication of *Origin of the Species* Darwin defended the idea of a creator-god as the First Cause, or ultimate source of life, but not directly responsible for new species. After the 1850s he rejected theism, at least in private. Maurice Mandelbaum, *History, Man, & Reason: A Study in Nineteenth-Century Thought* (Baltimore & London: Johns Hopkins Press, c1971), 85–87. After his death his literary heirs apparently suppressed correspondence that sounded too atheistic, while agreeing to publish letters expressing agnosticism. Gertrude Himmelfarb, *Darwin and the Darwinian Revolution* (Garden City: Doubleday Anchor, 1962), 384.

16.  This interpretation actually went far afield from Darwin's views on natural selection. In *Origin of the Species* Darwin warned against misconstruing his "metaphorical expressions" describing the forces of nature, a warning Muir read and underscored. See his marks beside an excerpt from *Origin of the Species* in *A Library of the World's Best Literature, Ancient and Modern*, XI (New York: The International Society, 1897), 4425, in John Muir Book Collection, HL, hereafter cited as JMC HL. As Stephen Jay Gould and others have noted, Darwin insisted that evolution tended only toward specialization, not progress. See Gould, *Ever Since Darwin: Reflections in Natural History* (New York: W. W. Norton, c1977), 34–38.

Muir and many other Darwinians gave natural selection a Lamarckian slant. Lamarck's theory, widely accepted before the publication of *Origin of the Species,* said evolution tended "towards greater complexity and perfection." Jean Baptiste Lamarck, as quoted in James Rachels, *Created from Animals: The Moral Implications of Darwinism* (Oxford & New York: Oxford Univ. Press, 1990), 14.

17.  Harry Thurston Peck, introduction to "Aesop," in *A Library of the World's Best Literature, Ancient and Modern*, LV, 202, JMC HL. See also Mary Allen, *Animals in American Literature* (Urbana: Univ. of Illinois, 1983), 3–4.

18.  Albert Borgmann, "The Nature of Reality and the Reality of Nature," a paper presented at a conference on "Reinventing Nature," University of California, at Santa Cruz, March 27, 1993.

19. Muir was disappointed to learn that even Emerson, the progenitor of Muir's own nature philosophy, distinguished between wilderness advocacy and total submission. Declining Muir's invitation to spend a week together in the Yosemite wilds, the aging Bostonian offered a pragmatic aphorism: "solitude . . . is a sublime mistress but an intolerable wife." Emerson to Muir, February 5, 1872, in William F. Badé, *The Life and Letters of John Muir*, I (Boston: Houghton Mifflin, 1923), 259–60.

20. Mighetto, "Science, Sentiment, and Anxiety," 33–37; Turner, *Reckoning with the Beast*, 60–77. Leo Marx explored the pastoral idea and its cultural implications in his classic study, *The Machine in the Garden: Technology and the Pastoral Ideal in America* (New York: Oxford Univ. Press, 1967).

21. The term comes from the title of a conference held at the University of California, Santa Cruz, March 26–28, 1993.

22. See Muir's margin marks and endnotes in *A Library of the World's Best Literature*, VI, 2615, JMC HL.

23. Carolyn Merchant, *The Death of Nature: Women, Ecology, and the Scientific Revolution* (New York: Harper & Row, 1989), 99–111, 192–93.

24. Ralph W. Emerson, *Prose Works*, v. 1 (Boston: Fields, Osgood, 1870), 269, in Beinecke Library, Yale University. This was Muir's copy, and the passage quoted is marked in Muir's hand.

25. Gray even called for the development of an "evolutionary teleology." See Himmelfarb, *Darwin and the Darwinian Revolution*, 390.

26. Rachels, *Created from Animals*, 3.

27. Charles Darwin, *Journal of Researches into the Natural History and Geology of the Countries Visited During the Voyage of the* H. M. S. Beagle *Round the World* (London: T. Nelson & Sons, 1891), 121, in JML, UOPWA.

28. Arthur O. Lovejoy, *The Great Chain of Being: A Study of the History of an Idea* (New York: Harper Torchbooks, c1936, 1960), especially pages 24–66, 183–207, 242–314. Stephen Jay Gould has summarized the biological fallacies of chain theory in *The Flamingo's Smile: Reflections in Natural History* (New York: W. W. Norton, c1985), 281–90.

29. See the paraphrase of Emerson in Muir's 1872 journal, as quoted in R. H. Limbaugh, "The Nature of Muir's Religion," *Pacific Historian*, 29 (Summer/Fall, 1985), 25.

30. *Scientific Papers of Asa Gray*, Vol. 1 (Boston & New York: Houghton, Mifflin, 1889), John Muir Library, in Holt-Atherton Library, University of the Pacific, hereafter cited as JML UOPWA.

31. Thomas Carlyle, *The Life of John Sterling* (London: Chapman & Hall, 1870), in JML, UOPWA.

32. Muir holograph endnote in Alfred Russell Wallace, *The World of Life: A Manifestation of Creative Power, Directive Mind and Ultimate Purpose* (New York: Moffat, Yard & Co., 1911), JML, UOPWA.

33. Muir holographic endnote in Nathaniel Hawthorne, *The Scarlet Letter* (Boston: Houghton Mifflin, 1884), in JML, UOPWA.

34. Samuel Taylor Coleridge, *The Table Talk and Omniana of Samuel Taylor Coleridge* (London: George Bell and Sons, 1888), 52, Muir endnotes, in JML UOPWA.

35. John Muir, advanced holograph draft fragments of Stickeen manuscript, p. 66, in JMP (microfilm), 42/09018.

36. Mighetto, "Science, Sentiment, and Anxiety," 37–42; "Wildlife Protection and the New Humanitarianism," *Environmental Review* 12 (Spring 1988): 37–41; Allen, *Animals in American Literature*, 5–6.

37. Henry S. Salt, "The Rights of Animals," *International Journal of Ethics* 10 (January 1900): 206.

38. In 1958 Judson McGehee argued that Muir's writing was not only anthropomorphic but indulged in a "careless falsification," the "pathetic fallacy" of attributing human emotions to insentient nature. However, said McGehee, the practice was common to many early nature writers, including Thoreau, and in most cases they lessened the harm by using qualifying words such as "seems" or "as if." McGehee, "The Nature Essay as a Literary Genre," 146–51. As one indicator of the change in emphasis that has occurred since the environmental movement of the 1960s, compare McGehee's criticism with the recent study by Max Oelschlaeger, who applauds Muir's perception that "even plants and inorganic matter" were "endowed with spirit." This "animistic vision" was a revolutionary insight, he says, and he argues that rediscovering the "Paleolithic mind"—which Muir exemplified—is essential if the postmodern world hopes to restore a balanced relationship between all objects in nature. Oelschlaeger, *The Idea of Wilderness* (New Haven: Yale University Press, c1991), 184–85, 344–53.

39. George S. Hellman, "Animals in Literature," *Atlantic Monthly* 87 (March 1901): 391–97.

40. See Muir's margin marks beside an excerpt from Griffin's *The Collegians*, as quoted in *A Library of the World's Best Literature*, XVII, 6703, JMC HL.

41. John Burroughs, *My Dog Friends*. ed. by Clara Barrus (Boston & NY: Houghton Mifflin, 1928), 76–77; "On Humanizing the Animals," *Century* 67 (March 1904): 780. Ironically, Henry Fairfield Osborn, who knew both Burroughs and Muir, claimed that Muir "did not humanize his birds and mammals as Burroughs did." Osborne, "The Racial Soul of John Burroughs," in *Public Meeting of the American Academy and the National Institute of Arts and Letters in Honor of John Burroughs* (New York: American Academy of Arts and Letters, 1922), 3.

42. For example, see Wesley Mills, *The Nature & Development of Animal Intelligence* (New York: Macmillan, 1898), 6–7. Studies of animal behavior moved from the field to the laboratory only with the development of modern comparative and experimental psychology after 1900. Robert M. Young, "Animal Soul," in *The Encyclopedia of Philosophy*, I (New York: Macmillan, 1967), 122–27; David McFarland, *The Oxford Companion to Animal Behavior* (Oxford & NY: Oxford Univ. Press, 1982), 310–11; Robert Boakes, *From Darwin to Behaviourism*, 136–75; Rachels, *Created from Animals*, 148–52.

43. John Burroughs, *The Summit of the Years* (Boston & NY: Houghton Mifflin, 1913), 167.

44. For a discussion of pre-Darwinian ethics, see *Ethics and Animals*, edited by Harlan B. Miller and William H. Williams (Clifton, NJ: Humana Press, 1983), esp. 2–14. The impact of Christian thinking on western development is briefly discussed in Limbaugh, "The Nature of John Muir's Religion," 16–29.

45. See, for example, Lynn White, Jr., "The Historical Roots of Our Ecologic Crisis," *Science*, v. 155 (March 10, 1967): 1207; Joseph Wood Krutch, as cited in Lawrence Buell, "The Thoreauvian Pilgrimage: The Structure of an American Cult," *American Literature* 61 (May 1989): 193.

46. Limbaugh, "The Nature of John Muir's Religion," 25–27; Bernard E. Rollin, *Animal Rights and Human Morality* (New York: Prometheus Books), 6–9.

47. John Passmore, "The Treatment of Animals," *Journal of the History of Ideas* 36 (April–May, 1975): 204–05; Albert G. A. Balz, "Cartesian Doctrine and the Animal Soul: An Incident in the Formation of the Modern Philosophical Tradition," in *Cartesian Studies* (New York:

Columbia Univ. Press, 1951), 109–16; Rollin, *Animal Rights and Human Morality*, 10–ll; Miller and Williams, eds., *Ethics and Animals*, 3, 6.

48. Robert M. Young, "Animal Soul," *The Encyclopedia of Philosophy*, vol. 1 (NY: MacMillan, 1967), 122–23.

49. Leonora C. Roselfield, *From Beast-Machine to Man-Machine: Animal Soul in French Letters from Descartes to La Mettrie*, new and enlarged ed. (New York: Octagon Books, 1968), 192.

50. Cosslett, *The 'Scientific Movement' and Victorian Literature* (Sussex: The Harvester Press, c1982), 7–29.

51. *The Encyclopedia of Philosophy*, Paul Edwards, editor in chief, III (New York: Macmillan & The Free Press, 1967), 399–402. Professor William D. Gunning, a Unitarian minister and Haeckel protege, toured the West Coast in 1878, but he shocked audiences with outrageous evolution stories, asserting, for instance, that Adam and Eve were black and covered with hair. His mockery of orthodox religion won few sympathizers. Asked his opinion of Gunning, Muir said not to waste time with such "poor game"; they will "destroy themselves" with lies. Letter, Muir to Annie K. Bidwell, 13 February 1878, JMP (microfilm), 3/01703.

52. Modern philosophers are still debating the ethical and moral ramifications. See Peter Singer, *Animal Liberation: A New Ethics for Our Treatment of Animals* (New York: New York Review, c1975), 2–9. Singer's controversial book attempted to strike a middle ground in the modern debate over animal rights, but his utilitarian argument has been challenged by some ethicists. See David Lamb, "Animal Rights and Liberation Movements," *Environmental Ethics* 4 (Fall 1982): 215–33.

53. Badé, *Life and Letters*, I, 42.

54. John Muir, AMS notebook [1897], p. 94, in JMP (microfilm) 33/01521.

55. Huxley, in a passage marked by Muir, quoted with approval a post-Darwinian essay discussing the biological linkage of primates and then carried the argument farther: "I may add the expression of my belief that the attempt to draw a psychical distinction is equally futile, and that even the highest faculties of feeling and of intellect begin to germinate in lower forms of life." Thomas H. Huxley, *Man's Place in Nature and Other Anthropological Essays* (New York: Appleton, 1894), 152, JML, UOPWA.

56. Nathaniel S. Shaler, *The Interpretation of Nature,* 4th ed. (Boston & New York: Houghton, Mifflin, 1895), 257, in JML UOPWA.

57. Robert Boakes, *From Darwin to Behaviourism: Psychology and the Minds of Animals* (Cambridge: Cambridge Univ. Press, 1984), 24–25.

58. George J. Romanes, *Animal Intelligence* (New York: D. Appleton, 1883), 10, in JML UOPWA. By World War I Romanes's views on various gradations of animal intelligence were widely accepted by the scientific community. A few years later Vernon Kellogg, a Stanford biologist who had known Muir, wrote a treatise along the same lines, describing the evolution of intelligence and the complementary influences of heredity and environment in determining the mental qualities of higher animals. Vernon L. Kellogg, *Mind and Heredity* (Princeton: Princeton Univ. Press, 1923).

59. In 1896 Muir gave the book to his eldest daughter on her fifteenth birthday. His inscription is revealing: "To Wanda, nurse & friend & lover of all her feeble fellow mortals . . . ."

60. Holograph endnote in ibid., JML UOPWA.

61. Ibid., p. 460.

62. Holograph endnote in ibid.

63. Cosslett, *The 'Scientific Movement' and Victorian Literature,* 36–37.

64. Henry S. Salt, *Animals' Rights Considered in Relation to Social Progress* (New York: Macmillan, 1894), 1–22. In 1908 Salt corresponded with Muir and sent him a copy of his most recent book, *On Cambrian and Cumbrian Hills.* It now resides with the Muir library collection at UOP. For Salt's importance in the humanitarian faction of the animal rights movement, see Lisa Mighetto, "Wildlife Protection and the New Humanitarianism," *Environmental Review* 12 (Spring 1988): 37–49.

65. Mighetto, *Muir Among the Animals* (San Francisco: Sierra Club Books, 1986), xx–xxii.

66. "Bears," holograph ms., ca. 1872, JMP (microfilm), 34/02018.

67. For example, see Linnie Marsh Wolfe's revised version of Muir's statement on bears in *John of the Mountains,* 82–83.

68. Muir holograph note in Bagehot, *Literary Studies (Miscellaneous Essays),* v. 3 (1895), in JML, UOPWA.

69. Ibid.

70. Brown, *Horae Subsecivae,* v. 2 (1889), in JML, UOPWA.

71. Eliot, *Wit and Wisdom* (1885), in JML, UOPWA.

72. Hawthorne, *The Scarlet Letter* (1884), in JML, UOPWA.

73. Brown, *Horae Subsecivae*, v. 1 (1889), in JML, UOPWA.

74. Muir holograph note in Hawthorne, *Septimius Felton, with an Appendix Containing The Ancestral Footstep* (Boston: Houghton Mifflin, 1884), in JML UOPWA.

75. John Muir, "Wild Wool," *Overland Monthly* 14 (May 1875): 361–66. See also "Wild Sheep of California," *Overland Monthly* 12 (April 1874): 358–363.

76. Muir holograph notes in [Stickeen] draft notebook 06474, JMP (microfilm), 33/011344. Muir used the words "dull" or "dullness" at least thirty-five different times in a variety of draft passages trying to describe the dog's character prior to crossing the ice bridge. See especially the endnotes in books by Hawthorne, Ruskin, and Taine in the Muir collection at the Holt-Atherton, and in Muir's 1896 draft notebook, JMP (microfilm), 33/01338–01384.

    Seventy years later, a bolder "scientist-populizer," William Beebe, lashed out at commercial breeders in a statement Muir could have written, but would not have published: "We breed monstrosities of canines, flatten their poor faces, shorten their legs to mere stumps, give them hyperthyroid eyes, strip them naked as the dawn or imbed them in such masses of hair that they can scarcely see; . . . make them permanent cowards or chronic fighters, waddlers, or mile-a-minuters." William Beebe, *Unseen Life of New York*, as quoted in McGehee, "The Nature Essay as a Literary Genre," 119.

77. John Muir holographic note in the endpages of Thomas Carlyle, *Wilhelm Meister's Apprenticeship and Travels* (London: Chapman & Hall, [n.d.]), vol. 1, in JML UOPWA.

78. Jonathan Bishop, *Emerson On the Soul* (Cambridge: Harvard Univ. Press, 1964), 19.

79. James F. Clarke, "Have Animals Souls?," *Atlantic Monthly* 34 (October 1874): 422.

80. In England, Victorian novelist Charles Kingsley led the literary opposition with *The Water Babies*. Leo J. Henkin, *Darwinism in the English Novel, 1860–1910: The Impact of Evolution on Victorian Fiction* (New York: Russell & Russell, 1963), 145–46.

81. *The Pocket Richard Jefferies, Being Passages Chosen from the Nature Writings of Jefferies* (Boston: Small, Maynard & Co., 1907), 48, in JML UOPWA.

82. Thomas H. Huxley, *Life and Letters of Thomas Henry Huxley*, I (New York: D. Appleton, 1900), 234, in JML UOPWA.

83. Vernon L. Kellogg, "Ernst Haeckel: Darwinist, Monist," *Popular Science Monthly* 76 (February 1910): 136–42; Thomas H. Huxley, "Are Animals Automatons?" *Popular Science Monthly* 5 (October 1874): 732–33. Peter Alan Dale, *In Pursuit of a Scientific Culture: Science, Art and Society in the Victorian Age* (Madison: Univ. of Wisconsin Press, c1989), 11–14.

84. See page 71 above.

85. Quoted in Max Müller, "The Impassable Barrier between Brutes and Man," *Classics in Biology*, ed. Sir S. Zuckerman (Edinburgh: Philosophical Library, Inc., 1960), 215.

86. Thomas Huxley, "Are Animals Automatons?" 730–32.

87. John Wilson, selections from "Noctes Ambrosianae," as quoted in *A Library of the World's Best Literature,* XXXIX, 16045, JMC HL.

88. Muir holograph passage in "An Adventure with a Dog and a Glacier," advanced draft fragments, JMP (microfilm), 42/09018.

89. Between January and June 1897 he prepared at least three different versions of the story, each progressively refining the immortality line until he had two guarded variants with which he could end the story. The 1897 version is quoted in the text. The second, simpler version, he used in the 1909 book: "To me Stickeen is immortal." JM holograph manuscripts, 42/09018, 42/09029, JMP (microfilm); "An Adventure with a Dog and a Glacier," *Century* 54 (September 1897), 776; *Stickeen* (Boston: Houghton Mifflin, 1909), 74.

90. *Memoirs of the Life of Sir Walter Scott, Bard,* III (Edinburgh: Adam & Charles Black, 1856), 209, in JMP UOPWA. In 1910, during the "nature faker" dispute over questionable evidence of animal intelligence reported by naturalists without scientific credentials, Muir replied to a reporter's inquiry: "What is the use of trying to prove that animals have souls or reason? I believe they have myself, and that we are all kin with them. . . .but as to controversy on such a subject, it would be valueless." *Los Angeles Examiner,* 1910, as quoted in William F. & Maymie B. Kimes, *John Muir: A Reading Bibliography* (Fresno: Panorama West Books, 1986), 156.

91. J. Donald Hughes, "The Environmental Ethics of the Pythagoreans," *Environmental Ethics* 2 (Fall 1980): 195–213.

92. Emerson wrote: "The transmigration of souls is not fable. I would it were; but men and women are only half human. Every animal of the barnyard, the field, and the forest, of the earth and of the waters that are under the earth, has contrived to get a footing and to leave the

print of its features and form in some one or other of these upright, heaven-facing speakers." Ralph W. Emerson, *Prose Works*, Vol. 1 (Boston: Fields, Osgood & Co., 1870), 201, in Beinecke Library, Yale. Thoreau had been even more enthusiastic, although like Muir his most radical views were not published in his lifetime. He had a "peculiar sympathy . . . with beasts and even with plants . . . " that derived in part " . . . from a belief that his soul had once inhabited a plant or animal." Raymond W. Adams, "Thoreau and Immortality," *Studies in Philology* 26 (January 1929): 63–66.

93. Muir holograph note in [Stickeen] manuscript 06474, JMP (microfilm), 33/01376.

94. Thomas Browne, *Religio Medici and Urn-burial* (London: J. M. Dent, 1896), 55, in JMC HL. As John Passmore has pointed out, metempsychosis was rejected in the West because of Aristotle's theory that "the soul is the form of the body" and hence could not transmigrate. Passmore, "The Treatment of Animals," 216.

95. Muir note in advanced draft of "An Adventure with a Dog and a Glacier," in JMP (microfilm), 43/09449.

96. Muir holograph note in *Horae Subsecivae,* vol. 1, JML UOPWA.

97. Muir holograph note in Carlyle, *History of Friedrich II*, vol. 2, JML UOPWA.

98. Muir draft passage in [Stickeen] manuscript, JMP (microfilm), 13/01357; *The Wit and Wisdom of George Eliot,* (Boston: Roberts Bros., 1885), in JML, UOPWA.

99. This is Muir's phrase as expressed in his notes at the back of Taine's *History of English Literature*. He tried various other versions. See endnotes in Carlyle's *The French Revolution*, vol. 1, and *Oliver Cromwell's Letters and Speeches*, vol. 1, as well as those in Eliot, *Wit and Wisdom*, and in the 1896 Stickeen draft. All are in JML UOPWA and JMP, Stickeen manuscript (microfilm), 33/01367.

100. It should be noted that Muir later restored many of R. U. Johnson's textual changes in a revised version published by Houghton-Mifflin in 1909 under Muir's original title, *Stickeen*.

# Five

# The Final Draft of 1897

Muir's letter to Robert Underwood Johnson on June 18, 1897, marked the completion of his most difficult composition. He had labored for years under the strain of developing the style and ideas his reading and reflection had generated. The result was an essay that he believed met the terms of his obligation to *Century Magazine* but at the same time was more than a simple dog story. Challenging both the conventions of his craft as a popular writer and the norms of popular culture, he mixed contemporary science with the best of Judaeo-Christian ethical tradition. With exquisite charm he wrote a glowing portrait of human and animal bonding, a spiritual fusion between two phylogenetically interrelated species, both with infinite capacity for joy and love.

The final version is here presented as faithfully as possible to the original manuscript that Muir submitted to *Century* in June of 1897. The initial text, written in ink, is located in the Muir Papers at the Holt-Atherton Library and can be clearly distinguished from both Johnson's editorial elisions and Muir's later changes in pencil. Each page of the 1897 version is numbered in parentheses, with footnotes indicating missing pages and the location of substitutions. Muir's shorthand spelling has been filled

*The title page of Muir's final draft. Note the change of title by Muir's editor, Robert Underwood Johnson.*

out where necessary for clarity, with added letters in braces { }. Minor mistakes in spelling and punctuation have been corrected without indication. In one or two instances elisions have been necessary to integrate text from the three different versions.

Unfortunately a few pages of the original draft have been lost. Parts of the text, therefore, have been partly reconstructed from advanced draft fragments. Johnson's editorial additions, where known, have been removed, and his deletions have been placed in brackets [ ] for easy identification. Muir himself restored some of them in 1908 when he was preparing a draft of the book published a year later. Footnotes at the end of bracketed segments indicate which portions deleted by Johnson Muir restored for the 1909 edition. Those not restored are bracketed but not footnoted. What follows, then, is the 1897 story essentially as Muir presented it for publication.

## *Stickeen*[1]

[(1) An insignificant looking little dog by the name of Stickeen once encountered a terrible adventure on one of the great glaciers of Alaska, in which all the mean disguises that hid his mind were stripped off, & then he became to me the most interesting & unforgettable of all the dogs I ever knew]

This happened in the summer of 1880. I then hired a crew of Indians & with Mr. Young, my former companion, set out from Fort Wrangel in a canoe to continue the exploration of the icy region of Southeastern Alaska, begun in the fall of 1879. After the necessary provisions, blankets, etc. had been collected & stowed away, & the Indians were in their places ready to dip their paddles, while a crowd of their friends were looking down from the wharf to bid them Goodluck & Goodbye,(2)[2] Mr. Young came aboard, followed by a little black dog that immediately made himself at home by curling up in a hollow among the baggage. I like dogs but this one seemed so small & dull & worthless I objected to his going & asked the missionary what he was taking him for. Such a helpless wisp of hair would only be in the way I said. You had better pass him up to one of the Indian boys on the wharf to be taken home to play with the children. This trip is not one for toy dogs. He will be rained & snowed on for weeks & require nursing & coddling like a baby. But the missionary assured me he would be no trouble at all, that he was a perfect wonder of a dog however silly he looked, could endure cold & hunger like a polar bear, was a capital sailor, could swim like a seal & was wondrous wise etc. etc. making out a list of virtues likely to make him the most interesting of the company. [And so strange to say he at length proved. For never in all my excursions have I gained so grand a lesson from man or beast as the one I got from Stickeen.]

[(3) But even his master did not half know him. As the Scotch say "You canna tell by the look of a frog how far he can jump." And we never know by what messenger Heaven is going to send gifts.]

Stickeen's ancestry was hopelessly doubtful. [He had no pretension to be considered above chance-bred dogs, & possessed no bright traits or accomplishments to make him desirable.] He was shortlegged, smooth haired, bunchy-bodied, & almost featureless; something like a muskrat. Though smooth his hair was rather long & silky, so that when the wind was at his back it ruffled, making him shaggy. His only noticeable features were keen dark eyes & a showy squirrelish tail which he carried curled forward nearly to his ears.

Mr. Young told me that when he was the size of a woodrat he was presented to (4)[3] Mrs. Young by an Irish prospector at Sitka & that when he arrived at Fort Wrangel

he was adopted by the Stickeen Indians as a new good luck
totem, named Stickeen & became a favorite with the tribe.
On our trip he soon proved himself a queer character, odd,
concealed, withdrawn, independent, keeping inscrutably
quiet & doing many unexplainable things that drew my
attention & piqued curiosity [until on the great storm day
when he was compelled to pass thru the valley of the shadow
of death all obscurity was stripped off mind & soul, he was
revealed & became immortal to me.] Sailing week after week
through the long intricate channels among the innumerable
islands of the coast he spent the dull days curled up in the
baggage in sluggish ease motionless & apparently as
unobserving as a hibernating marmot. But I discovered that
somehow he always knew what was going forward. When
the Indians were about to shoot at ducks or seals, or when
anything interesting was to be seen along the shore, then he
would rest his chin on the edge of the canoe & calmly look
(5) out. And when he heard us talking about making a
landing he roused himself to see what sort of a place we were
coming to, & made ready to jump overboard & swim ashore
as soon as the canoe neared the beach. Then, with a vigorous
shake to get rid of the brine in his hair, he went into the
woods to hunt small game. But though always the first out of
the canoe, he was always the last to get into it. When we
were ready to start he could never be found, & refused to
come to our call. We soon found out, however, that though
we could not see him at such times he saw us, & from the
cover of the briars & huckleberry bushes in the fringe of the
woods was watching the canoe with wary eye. For as soon as
we were fairly off he came in sight, trotting down the beach,
plunged into the surf, & swam after us, knowing well that we
would cease rowing & take him in.

(6) When the little contrary vagabond came alongside
he was lifted by the neck, held at arms length a moment to

drip, & dropped aboard. We tried to cure him of this trick by compelling him to swim farther before stopping for him, but this did no good. The longer he swam the better he seemed to like it. Though capable of most spacious idleness, he was always ready for excursions or adventures of any sort. When the Indians went into the woods for a deer, Stickeen was sure to be at their heels, provided I had not yet left camp. For though I never carried a gun he always followed me, forsaking the hunting Indians, & even his own master, to share my wanderings. The days that were too stormy for sailing I spent in the woods, or on the mountains or glaciers (7)[4] wherever I chanced to be & Stick always insisted on following me, gliding thro the dripping huckleberry bushes & prickly panax & rubus tangles like a fox scarce stirring their close-set branches, wading & wallowing through snow, swimming ice-cold streams, jumping logs & rocks & the crusty hummocks & crevasses of cascading gl{acier}s with the patience & endurance of a determined mtneer never tiring or getting discouraged. Once he followed me over a gl{acier}. The rough melting surface cut his feet until every step was marked with blood. But he trotted on with Ind{ian} fortitude until I noticed his pain & took pity on him. First I carried him awhile, then made him a set of moccasins out of a handkerchief. But he never asked assistance or made any complaint as if like a philosopher he had learned that without hard work & suffering there could be no pleasure worth having . . .

[(8) One dark rainy night we landed at the mouth of a salmon-stream when the water was vividly phosphorescent, & while camp was being made I paddled with one of the Indians to the foot of a rapid to catch a few of the salmon that were then running in crowding excited multitudes. As we neared the rapids, suddenly in the gulf of ebon darkness walled in & overarched by the dense forest we saw a portentous wedge of light on the water that seemed to be made by some mysterious leviathan of the deep that was pursuing us, clearing its impetuous way over the surging throng of fishes. On it came until we fancied we should see the monster's head dividing the luminous water, which streamed back from it in the darkness like the tail of a comet. But the monster was only Stickeen, who on hearing the canoe paddled off had plunged in & followed; for to this adventurer day & night land & water were the same. ]⁵

Yet nobody knew (9) what he was good for. He seemed to meet danger & hardships without reason, insisted on having his own way in everything, never obeyed an order, & the hunters could never set him on anything against his will or make him fetch anything that was shot. I tried hard to make his acquaintance, guessing there must be something in him, but he was as cold as a glacier, & about as invulnerable to fun, though his master assured me that he played at home, & in some measure conformed to the usages of civilization. His equanimity was so immovable it seemed due to unfeeling ignorance. Let the weather blow & roar, he was tranquil as a stone, & no matter what advances you made, scarce a glance or tail-wag would you get for your pains. No superannuated mastiff or bulldog grown (10) old in office surpassed this soft midget in stoic dignity. [He was the wildest gentle dog I ever saw. His education was thin & lay lightly over his main traits derived from the wilderness. In the interior of Alaska the Indian dogs are all serious, on account of hunger & hard work. By some of the tribes on the Yukon they are made beasts of burden as soon as they can carry a pound or two. Old & young are furnished with saddle-bags. Heavy-laden & abused, with them life is literally a burden, & natural playfulness is speedily quenched. Life is a serious matter with Eskimo dogs also. Never have I seen old stage horses pull more soberly than did the wolfish dogs that drew our sleds over the ice of the Arctic Ocean. Stickeen's hunting habits & his trick of hiding when we were leaving camp may have been derived from ancestors that tried to avoid their loads by refusing to be caught, & were fed only after something had been killed. He knew most of the creatures that haunt the woods especially the small hair ones—mice, weasels, squirrels, marmots etc—which he hunted at every (11) opportunity, prowling about old logs, rocks, & the roots of trees in a strikingly wild stealthy way; darting keen glances through the underbrush, & lifting his feet with needless caution on the soundless moss; pawing & poking with grave industry, never trifling with the game he killed, but without yelp or growl quickly ending the job. Nothing escaped his notice—flocks of swans on their long journeys a mile high in the air, geese & ducks passing over from one feeding ground to another, loons, gulls, eagles, crows, plovers-noisy screaming chattering people feeding, fighting, playing, he knew them all, but kept himself dark. At mealtimes he came forward for bread bacon etc, & what he liked best, bits of salmon & venison, over which smacking his lips he could hardly conceal his pleasure, always preferring to take food from my hand—another queer notion. From most common faults he was free. He was immutably decorous & dull, dainty in his habits, & never begged, stole, whined, or got in the way. But in the midst of this soft tranquil behavior he was prodigiously obstinate & held on to his small whims & purposes with invincible grip.

He was particular about his beds, & no dog had better ones, for all the mossy ground was a bed. A hollow (12) at the foot of a tree was a favorite place. There curled up with his warm tail drawn around his toes & nose his comfort was complete. In stormy weather he accepted a place in the tent, always lying by me instead of his master. Why, nobody knew.

When we came to Indian villages he hardly noticed
other dogs, & was careful to avoid fights. Yet he was not
lacking in courage. Nothing on my rambles daunted him &
when the waves broke on the shore, making landing difficult,
he jumped into the seething foam like an otter. He enjoyed all
kinds of storms & as for mere rain he flourished in it like a
vegetable.] He sometimes reminded me of those plump,
squat, unshakable cactuses of the Arizona deserts that give no
sign of feeling. A true child of the wilderness, holding the
even tenor of his hidden life with the silence & serenity of
Nature, he never displayed a trace of the elfish vivacity & fun
of the terriers & collies that we all know, nor of their touch-
ing affection & devotion. Like children, most small dogs beg
to be loved & allowed to love, but Stickine seemed a very
Diogenes, asking only to be let alone. [He kept his heart &
thoughts private. Even his limbs were bunched into invisibil-
ity. He seemed neither old nor young.] In his eyes his (13)
strength lay. They looked as old as the hills & as young & as
wild. I never tired looking into them. It was like looking into
a landscape. But they were small & rather deep set & had no
explaining puckers around them to give out particulars. I was
accustomed to look into the faces of plants & animals, & I
watched the little Sphinx more & more keenly as an interesting study. But there is no estimating the wit & wisdom
concealed & latent in our lower fellow mortals until made
manifest by profound experiences; for it is by suffering that
dogs as well as saints are developed & made perfect.

[How little we know of the thoughts & feelings of
animals, even of those we see every day; but always the more
we learn of them the nearer to ourselves we find them. No
wonder so many believe or half believe the Pythagorean
notion of transmigration of souls. Occasionally some quick
gleams of intelligence from Stickeen's eyes suggested he might

be some old Hindoo philosopher. Certainly he had a good sound mind & soul in him, & on his great trial day he found his voice & outpreached all the dogs I ever heard & even his master, on the very oneness of all God's creatures great & small, vertical & horizontal.

(14) Is it not truly marvelous that animals in such lively varied multitudes should be with us & yet remain so darkly apart from us. As a whole we know about as little of them in their inner life & conversation as we do of the inhabitants of other stars. Children, savages, poets & backwoodsmen know them best. "If they could only talk" we say. But they do in a universal language no Babel has ever confused; & the gift to them of articulate speech would probably leave us about as far apart as before. How much do we make of speech in knowing each other.

In our studies of animals almost all their intelligence is called "Instinct," & how much ignorance is complacently & arrogantly slumped into & covered up in that one useful word! It is darker & more capacious than the widest & most unfathomable glacier crevasse. In our great adventure Stickeen suffered & rejoiced from the same (15) causes as I did; thought reasoned & reached the same conclusions, & I have since found far less use for that dark word.

In proportion as civilization advances the range of our sympathy seems to diminish. Even in religion animals are all but lost sight of. We throw our heavens open to every vertical mammal but close them against the horizontal ones. Some Indians are more charitable. They allow their dogs to follow them into their happy hunting grounds. I believe there is a hereafter for some of God's other people as well as for Jews & Gentiles, & that measured by love some dogs may be great even in heaven. With Burns we may well sympathize with the daisy & wee mousie & with all our fellow mortals however

lowly. We would thus, it seems to me, gain much & lose
nothing.]

(16) After we had explored the glaciers of the Sum
Dum & Tahkoo Inlets, we sailed through Stephen's Passage
into Lynn Canal, & thence through Icy Strait into Cross
Sound, looking for unexplored inlets leading toward the ice
fountains of the Fairweather Range. While the tide was in
our favor, in Cross Sound we were accompanied by a fleet of
icebergs from Glacier Bay drifting out to the ocean. Slowly
we crawled around Vancouver's Pt. Wimbleton, our frail
canoe tossed & heaved like a feather on the massive swells
coming in past Cape Spenser. For miles the sound is bounded
by precipitous cliffs which looked terribly stern in the gloomy
weather. Had our canoe been crushed or upset we could have
gained no landing here, for the cliffs, high as those of
Yosemite, sink perfectly sheer into deep water. Eagerly we
scanned the immense wall for the first sign of an opening, all
of us anxious except Stickeen, who dozed in peace or gazed
dreamily at the tremendous precipices when he heard us
talking about them. At length we (17) discovered the en-
trance of what is now called Taylor Bay, & about five o'clock
reached the head of it & encamped near the front of a large
glacier, which extends as an abrupt barrier all the way across
from wall to wall of the inlet, a distance of three of four
miles. [Great however as it is, this glacier no longer sends off
icebergs. It is in the first stage of decadence, & its front is
separated from the waters of the bay by a low plain of
washed moraine material. The walls of the inlet are high but
they are not sculptured into very striking forms, & only two
tributary glaciers of large size come forward to break their
massive simplicity.]

[While camp was being made, Joe, the best hunter of
the party, climbed the mountain wall on the east side in

pursuit of wild goats but found only a bear. Mr. Young & I
sauntered over the moraine to the front of the glacier & were
surprised to find that it had recently advanced.][6]

[(18, 19)[7] The Indians regard glaciers as living creatures, & are careful not to offend them as they crawl on their
way devouring the woods & rocks. The Hoona tribe, as we
afterwards learned, know very well that this one had recently
advanced about a mile, for it flows across the mouth of a
stream on the west side from which for time immemorial a
branch of the tribe had obtained their yearly supplies of
salmon. This disastrous advance was supposed to be a
punishment & being anxious to appease the wrath of the
gods & get them to withdraw the damming glacier, they
consulted their Shamans, who advised them to kill & offer in
sacrifice a number of their best slaves. This was done; but the
precious salmon-stream is still dammed, & the sacrificial
blood was shed in vain.

Darkness put an end to these first observations, but on
the way back to camp] I planned a grand excursion for the
morrow.

(20, 21)[8] I awoke early, called not only by the glacier
but also by a storm. Rain, mixed with trailing films of scud
& the ragged drawn-out nether surfaces of gray clouds, filled
the inlet & was sweeping forward in one thick passionate
horizontal flood, as if it were all passing over the country
instead of falling on it. Everything was streaming with life &
motion—woods, rocks, waters, & the sky. The main peren-
nial streams were booming, & hundreds of new ones, born of
the rain, were descending in gray & white cascades on either
side of the inlet, fairly streaking their rocky slopes, & roaring
like the sea. I had intended making a cup of coffee before
starting, but when I heard the storm I made haste to join it;
for in storms Nature has always something extra-fine to

show us, & if we have wit to keep in right relations to it the danger is hardly more than in homekeeping & we can go on singing with the old Norsemen "The blast of the tempest aids our oars the hurricane is our servant & drives us whither we wish to go." So I just put a piece of bread in my pocket & pushed out. Mr Y & the Inds were asleep, & so I hoped was Stickine. [But how could I get away without that queer horizontal mortal.] I had not gone a dozen rods ere he left his warm bed & came boring through the blast after me. That a man should welcome storms to see & hear their wild motion & go forth to see God making landscapes is reasonable enough. But this poor wisp of a dog so pathetically small, what fascination could be found in dismal weather to draw him from his bed. [What could have moved his imagination . . . ]

[(22) Surely some inner fire that we know nothing about must have burned in him —something akin to human enthusiasm for scenery or geology. Anyhow on he came through the choking blast breakfastless.][9] I stopped, turned my back to the wind, & gave him a good dissuasive talk. "Now, don't," I said, shouting to make myself heard in the storm —"Now don't Stickeen. What has got into your queer noddle now? You must be daft. This wild day has nothing for you. Go back to camp & keep warm. There is no game abroad, nothing but cold weather & ice & rocks. Not a foot or wing is stirring. Wait & get a good breakfast with your master, & be sensible for once. I can't feed you or carry you, & this storm will kill you." But Nature, it seems, was at the bottom of the affair, & she gains her ends with dogs as well as men, making us do as she likes, driving us on her ways however rough, [thrashing us like a Scotch schoolmaster,] [& all but killing us at times to get her lessons (23) into us.][10] So after ordering him back again & again to ease my conscience,

I saw he was not to be shaken off. As well might the earth shake off the moon. I had once led his master into trouble, when he fell on one of the topmost jags of a mountain & dislocated his arms; now the turn of his humble companion was coming [like fate] He just stood there in the wind, drenched & blinking, saying doggedly, "Where thou goest I will go." So I told him to come on if he must, & gave him a piece of the bread I had put in my pocket for breakfast. Then we pushed on in company, & thus began the most memorable of all my wild days.

[We wandered in perfect freedom with the storm letting its hearty tides play over us, feeling the heartbeats of Nature with far less discomfort than home-keepers could guess. While the pleasure of seeing Nature at work driving everything into place with dance & song in passionate enthusiasm, only those who have enjoyed it can know it.]

(24) The level flood, driving straight in our faces, thrashed & washed us wildly until we got into the shelter of the trees & ice-cliffs on the east side of the glacier, where we rested & listened & looked on in comfort. The exploration of the glacier was my main object, but the wind was too high to allow excursions over its open surface, where one might be dangerously shoved while balancing for a jump on the brink of a crevasse. In the meantime the storm was a fine study. Here the end of the glacier, descending over an abrupt swell of resisting rock about five hundred feet high, leans forward & falls in majestic ice-cascades. And as the storm came down the glacier from the north, Stickeen & I were beneath the main current of the blast, while favorably located to see & hear it.

(25) A broad torrent, draining the side of the glacier, swollen by scores of new streams from the mountains, was now rolling bowlders along its rocky channel between the glacier & the woods with thudding, bumping, muffled

sounds, rushing towards the bay with tremendous energy, as
if in haste to get out of the mountains, the waters above &
beneath calling to each other, & all to the ocean, their home.
Looking southward from our shelter, we had this great
torrent on our left; with mossy woods on the mountain slope
above it, the glacier on our right, the wild cascading portion
of it forming a multitude of towers, spires, & flat-topped
battlements, seen through the trees, & smooth gray gloom
ahead. I tried to draw the marvelous scene in my notebook—(26)[11] [the immense ice towers, the leaning trees
beneath & beside them. . . .] The rain fell on my page however I tried to shelter it, & my sketch seemed miserably
untelling. [The colors of the leaves & mossy lichened rocks &
trunks were brightened by the rain & the trees & bushes gave
forth a fine fresh smell & everything was throbbing &
singing. The lower currents of the storm were broken &
subdued in the intricacies of the woods & rocks & ice-cliffs
& wandered hither [&] thither in gentle whispering wafts &
swirls carressing & comforting the rubus & huckleberry
bushes & now & then turning some of the fronds of the ferns
& showing their fruit-dotted undersides, just as little low
voiced rills slip out from the margins of the boisterous
torrents to cheer & refresh the flowers on their banks. And
from beneath the level oversweeping rain flood separate
drops came gently down (27) . . . these gentle undertones
blending with the all embracing roaring flood in one enthusiastic psalm—the art of God bringing music from everything—even from rocks & ice as if each crag & spike were a
reed in delicate tune. All the storm-work was love work. The
world was being made. It was still morning, & the song of
creation was sounding over the young wilderness.]

   When the wind began to abate I pushed up along the
east side of the glacier. All the trees standing on the edge of
the woods were barked & bruised, showing high ice-mark in

a very telling way, while tens of thousands of those that had stood for centuries on the bank of the glacier farther out lay crushed & being crushed. In many places I could see down fifty feet or so beneath the margin of the glacier mill where trunks from one to two feet in diameter were being ground to pulp against outstanding rock ribs & bosses of the bank. About three miles above the (28) front of the glacier I climbed to the surface of it by means of axe-steps made easy for Stickeen, & as far as the eye could reach the level, or nearly level, glacier stretched away indefinitely beneath the gray sky, a seemingly boundless prairie of ice. The rain continued, which I did not mind, but a tendency to fogginess in the drooping clouds made me hesitate about venturing far from land. No trace of the west shore was visible, & in case the misty clouds should settle, or the wind again become violent, I feared getting caught in a tangle of crevasses. Lingering undecided, watching the weather, I sauntered about on the crystal sea. For a mile or two out I found the ice remarkably safe. The marginal crevasses were mostly narrow while the few wider ones were easily avoided by passing around them, & the clouds began to open here & there. Thus encouraged, I at (29) last pushed out for the other side, for Nature can make us do anything she likes, luring us along appointed ways for the fulfillment of her plans. At first we made rapid progress & the sky was not very threatening, while I took bearings occasionally with a pocket compass to enable me to retrace my way more surely in case the storm should become blinding, but the structure lines of the ice were my main guide. Toward the west side we came to a closely crevassed section in which we had to make long narrow tacks & doublings, tracing the edges of tremendous longitudinal crevasses, many of which were from twenty to thirty feet wide, & perhaps from one thousand to two thousand feet deep, beautiful & awful. In working a way

through them I was severely cautious, but Stickeen came one
as unhesitating as the flying clouds. Any crevasse that I could
(30) jump so could he without halting to examine it. The
weather was bright & dark, mostly dark, with quick flashes
of summer & winter close together. When the clouds opened
& the sun shone the glacier was seen from shore to shore,
with a bright array of encompassing mountains partly
revealed, wearing the clouds as garments, black in the
middle, burning on the edges, & the whole crystal prairie
seemed to burst into a bloom of iris colors from myriads of
crystals. Then suddenly all the glorious show would be
smothered in gloom. But Stickeen seemed to care for none of
these things, bright or dark, nor for the beautiful wells filled
to the brim with water so pure it was nearly invisible, the
rumbling grinding moulins, or quick, flashing, glinting,
swirling streams in frictionless channels of living ice. Nothing
seemed novel to him. He showed neither caution nor
curiousity. [Crevasses six to eight feet wide he jumped with so
quick decision he did not seem to look at them at all.]

(31) His courage was so unwavering it seemed due to
dullness of perception, as if he were only blindly bold, & I
warned him that he might slip or fall short. [His bunchy body
seemed all one skipping muscle, & his peg legs appeared to
be jointed only at the top.]

We gained the west shore in three or four hours; the
width of the glacier here being about seven miles. Then I
pushed northward to see as far back as possible into the
fountains of the Fairweather mountains in case the clouds
should rise. The walking was easy along the margin of the
forest, which of course, like that on the other side, had been
invaded & crushed by the swollen glacier.

In an hour or so, after passing a massive headland we
came suddenly on a branch of the glacier which in the form
of a magnificent ice-cascade two miles wide was pouring over

the rim of the main basin in a westerly direction, its surface broken into wave-shaped blades & shattered blocks suggesting the wildest updashing heaving plunging hurrying motion of a great river cataract. Tracing it down (32)[12] three or four miles, I found that it discharged into a fresh-water lake, filling it with icebergs.

I would gladly have followed the lake outlet to tidewater; but the day was already far spent, & the threatening sky warned me to make haste on the return trip to get off the ice before dark. When we were about two miles from the west shore the clouds dropped misty fringes, & snow soon began to fly. Then I began to feel anxiety as to finding a way through the intricate network of crevasses we had entered. Stickeen showed no fear. He was still the same silent, sufficient, uncomplaining Indian philosopher. When the storm darkness fell he kept close behind me. ['Tis said that animals have instincts that forewarn them of danger which man dulled by civilization has lost.

(33) But of the supreme danger now drawing nigh Stickeen seemed unconscious until suddenly confronted with it.] The snow warned us to make haste but at the same time hid our way. At rare intervals the clouds thinned, & mountains looming in the gloom frowned & quickly vanished. I pushed on as best I could jumping innumerable crevasses, & traveling a mile in doubling up & down in the turmoil of chasms & dislocated masses of ice, for every hundred rods or so of direct advance. After an hour or two of this work we came to a series of longitudinal crevasses of appalling width like immense furrows. These I traced with firm nerve excited & strengthened by the danger, making wide jumps, poising cautiously on their dizzy edges after cutting hollows for my feet ere making the spring, to avoid slipping or any uncertainty on the farther sides where only one trial is granted— exercise at once frightful & inspiring. Stickeen flirted [his

little bunch of body] across every gap I jumped, seemingly
without effort. Many a mile we thus traveled mostly up &
down, making but little real headway in crossing, running
most of the time instead of walking, as the danger of (34)[13]
spending the night on the glacier became threatening. No
doubt we could have weathered the storm for one night, & I
faced the chance of being compelled to do so; but we were
hungry & wet, & the north wind thick with snow, was
bitterly cold, & of course that night would have seemed a
long one. Stickeen gave me no concern. He was still the
wonderful inscrutable philosopher able for anything. I could
not see far enough to judge in which direction the best route
lay, & had simply to grope my way in the snow-choked air &
ice. Again & again I was put to my mettle, but Stickeen
followed easily, nerves of course growing more unflinching as
the dangers thickened; so it always is with mountaineers. [By
tracing the crevasses up or down that were too wide to jump
I usually found that they narrowed within a distance of half a
mile, but we occasionally crossed the longer & wider ones by
sliver-like bridges twenty or thirty feet long, some of them
narrow & sharp like knife blades. These last I had to straddle
& grip with my knees, cutting off the sharp edges as I
progressed & leaving them about four (35) inches wide, &
flat or a little hollow in the centre to enable Stickeen to
follow, & he did follow me over these nerve trying bridges
without showing either fear or caution. Every difficult
crevasse of this sort I hoped would be the last. But on the
contrary they became more intricate & wider as we advanced. I doggedly persevered knowing the worst would only
be a nights dancing on a flat spot to keep from freezing.] At
length our way was barred by a very wide & straight crevasse, which I traced rapidly northward a mile or so without
finding a crossing or hope of one; then southward down the
glacier about as far to where it united with another crevasse.

In all this distance of perhaps two miles there was only one place where I could possible jump it, but the width of this jump was nearly the utmost I dared attempt, while the danger of slipping on the farther side was so great I was loathe to try it. Furthermore, the side I was on was about a foot higher than the other, & even with this advantage it seemed danger-ously wide. One is liable to underestimate the width of crevasses when the magnitudes in general are great.

(36) I therefore measured this one again & again until satisfied I could jump it if necessary, but that in case I should be compelled to jump back to the higher side I might fail. Now a cautious mountaineer seldom takes a step on un-known ground that seems at all dangerous that he cannot take back in case he should be stopped by unseen obstacles ahead. This is the rule of mountaineers who live long, & though in haste, I compelled myself to sit down & deliberate ere I broke it. Retracing my devious path in imagination as if it were drawn on a chart I saw that I was recrossing the glacier a mile or two farther upstream & was entangled in a section I had not before seen. Would I risk this dangerous jump, or try to regain the woods on the west shore, make a fire, & have only hunger to endure while waiting for a new day? I had already crossed so broad a tangle of dangerous ice I saw it would be difficult to get back to the woods through the thickening gloom while the ice just beyond the present barrier seemed more promising, & the east shore was now perhaps about as near as the west. I was therefore eager to go on. But this wide jump was (37) a tremendous obstacle. At length, because of the dangers already behind me, I deter-mined to venture against those that might be ahead, jumped, & landed well, but with so little to spare that I more than ever dreaded being compelled to take that jump back from the lower side. Stickeen followed, making nothing of it. But

within a distance of a few hundred yards we were stopped
again by the widest crevasse yet encountered. Of course I
made haste to explore it, hoping all might yet be well. About
three fourths of a mile upstream it united with the one we
had just crossed, as I feared it would. Then tracing it down, I
found it joined the other great crevasse at the lower end also,
maintaining a width of forty to fifty feet. We were on an
island about two miles long, & from one hundred to three
hundred yards wide, with two barely possible ways of escape,
one by the way we came, the other by an almost inaccessible
sliver bridge that crossed the larger crevasse from near the
middle (38) of the island! After tracing the brink I ran back
to the sliver bridge & cautiously studied it. Crevasses, caused
by strains from variations of the rate of motion of different
parts of the glacier & convexities in the channel, are mere
cracks when they first open, so narrow as hardly to admit the
blade of a pocketknife, & widen gradually according to the
extent of the strain. Now some of these cracks are inter-
rupted like the cracks in wood, & in opening, the strip of ice
between overlapping ends is dragged out, & if the flow of the
glacier there is such that no strain is made on the sliver, it
maintains a continuous connection between the sides, just as
the two sides of a silvered crack in wood are connected. Some
crevasses remain open for years, & by the melting of their
sides continue to increase in width long after the opening
strain has ceased; while the sliver bridges, level on top at first
& perfectly safe, are at length melted to thin knife-edged
blades, the upper portion being most exposed to the weather;
& since the exposure (39) is greatest in the middle they at
length curve downward like the cables of suspension bridges.
This one was evidently very old, for it had been wasted until
it was the worst bridge I ever saw. The width of the crevasse
was here about fifty feet, & the sliver crossing diagonally was

about seventy feet long, was depressed twenty five or thirty feet in the middle, & the upcurving ends were attached to the sides, eight or ten feet below the surface of the glacier. Getting down the nearly vertical wall to the end of it & up the other side were the main difficulties, & they seemed all but insurmountable. Of the many perils encountered in my walks none seemed so plain & stern & merciless as this. And it was presented when we were wet to the skin & hungry, the sky dark with snow, & the night near, & we had to fear the disturbing action of the wind in any movement we might make [& the snow in our eyes.] But we were forced to face it. It was a tremendous necessity.

(40) Beginning, not immediately above the sunken end of the bridge but a little to one side, I cut nice hollows on the brink for my knees to rest in. Then leaning over with my short handled axe cut a step sixteen or eighteen inches below, which on account of the wall was shallow. That step however was well made, its floor sloped slightly inward & formed a good hold for my heels. Then slipping, cautiously upon it, & crouching as low as possible, with my left side twisted toward the wall, I steadied myself with my left hand in a slight notch, while with the right I cut other steps & notches in succession, holding myself in delicate poise guarding against glinting of the axe, for life & death was in every stroke, & in the niceness of finish of every hold. After the end of the bridge was reached & it was a delicate thing to poise on a little platform I had chipped on its upcurving end, & bending over the slippery surface get astraddle of it. Crossing was (41) easy, cutting off the sharp edge with careful strokes, & hitching forward a few inches at a time, keeping my balance with my knees pressed against its sides. The tremendous abyss I ignored. The surface of that blue sliver was then all the world. But the most trying part of the adventure was

to rise from the safe straddling position on that slippery strip
of ice, & cutting a ladder in the face of the wall, chipping,
climbing, holding on with feet & fingers in mere notches
One's whole body is eye at such times, & common skill &
fortitude are replaced by power beyond our call or knowledge. Never before had I been so long under deadly strain.
How I got up that cliff at the end of the bridge I never could
tell. The thing seemed to have been done by somebody else. I
never had contempt of death, though in the course of my
explorations I oftentimes felt that to meet (42) one's fate on a
mountain, in a grand cañon, or in the heart of a crystal
glacier would be blessed as compared with death from
disease, mean accident in a street, or from a sniff of sewer
gas, etc. but the sweetest cleanest death set thus glaringly
clear before us is hard enough to face, even though feeling
gratefully sure that we have already had happiness enough
for a dozen lives, [& ought to be able to say Thank You God,
& go.]

    But poor Stickeen, the wee silky sleekit beastie, think of
him! When I decided to try the bridge & was on my knees
cutting away the rounded brow, he came behind me, pushed
his head past my shoulder, looked down & across, scanned
the sliver & its approaches with those queer eyes, then
looked me in the face with a startled air of surprise &
concern, & began to mutter & whine, saying as plainly as if
speaking with words (43) "Surely, you are not going to cross
here." This was the first time I had seen him look deliberately
into a crevasse or into my face with a speaking look. That he
should have recognized & appreciated the danger at the first
glance showed wonderful sagacity. Never before had the
quick daring midget seemed to know that ice was slippery or
that there was such a thing as danger anywhere. His looks &
tones of voice when he began to complain & speak his fears

were so human that I unconsciously talked to him as I would
to a boy, & in trying to calm his fears perhaps in some
measure moderated my own. "Hush your fears, my boy," I
said, "we will get across safely, though it is not going to be
easy. No right way is easy in this rough world. We must risk
our lives to save them. At the worst we can only slip, & then
how grand a grave we will have, & bye & bye our nice bones
will do good in the terminal moraine."

(44) But my sermon was far from reassuring him: he
began to cry, & after taking another piercing look at the
tremendous gulf, ran away in desperate excitement seeking a
crossing for himself. By the time he got back, baffled of
course, I had made a step or two. I dared not look back, but
he made himself heard; & when he saw that I was certainly
crossing here he cried aloud in despair. The danger was
enough to daunt anybody, but it seems wonderful that he
should have been able to so justly weight & appreciate it. No
mountaineer could have seen the danger quicker or judged it
more wisely, discriminating between real & apparent peril. [I
suppose we are always in peril though most of it is mercifully
hidden. Here it was savagely plain. "The ill that's wisely
feared," it is said, "is half withstood." Heaven knows we
feared it enough.]

After I had gained the other side he screamed louder
than ever, & after running (45) back & forth in vain search
for a way of escape, he would return to the brink of the
crevasse above the bridge moaning & groaning as if in the
bitterness of death. Could this be the silent philosophic
Stickeen? I shouted encouragement, telling him the bridge
was not so bad as it looked, that I had left it flat for his feet,
& he could walk it as easily as he had many others. But he
was afraid to try it. Strange so small an animal should be
capable of such big, wise fears. [He became a very poet &

prophet of misery.] I called again & again in a reassuring
tone to come on & fear nothing, that he could come if he
would only try. Then he would hush for a moment, look
again at the bridge & shout his unshakable conviction that he
could never, never come that way; & lie back in despair,
howling "Oh-oo what a place! No-o-o, I can never go-oo
down there!" (46) His natural composure & courage had
vanished utterly in a tumultuous storm of fear. Had the
danger been less his distress would have seemed ridiculous.
But in this gulf—a huge yawning sepulchre—big enough to
take in & hold everybody in the territory—lay the shadow of
death, & his heartrending cries might well have called
Heaven to his help. Perhaps they did. So hidden before, he
was transparent now, & one could see the workings of his
mind like the movements of a clock out of its case. His voice
& gestures were perfectly human & his hopes & fears
unmistakably expressed, while he seemed to understand every
word of mine. I was troubled at the thought of leaving him. It
seemed impossible to get him to venture. To compel him to
try by fear of being left I started off as if leaving him to his
fate, & disappeared (47) back of a hummock, but this did no
good, he only lay down & cried [more pitifully & louder] So
after hiding a few minutes I went back to the brink of the
crevasse & in a severe tone of voice shouted across to him
that now I must certainly leave him. I could wait no longer,
& that if he would not come, all I could promise was that I
would return to seek him next day; but warned him that if he
went back to the woods the wolves would kill him, &
finished by urging him once more by words & gestures to
come on. He knew very well what I meant, & at last with the
courage of despair, hushed & breathless he lay down on the
brink in the hollow I had made for my knees, pressed his
body against the ice to get the advantage of the friction,

gazed into the first step, put his (48) little feet together & slid them slowly down into it, bunching all four in it & almost standing on his head. Then without lifting them he slowly worked them over the edge of the step & down into the next & the next in succession in the same way, & gained the bridge. Then lifting his feet with the regularity & slowness of the vibrations of a seconds pendulum, as if counting & measuring 1,2,3, holding himself in dainty poise, & giving separate attention to each little step, he gained the foot of the cliff, at the top of which I was kneeling to give him a lift should he get within reach. Here he halted in dead silence, & it was here I feared he might fail, for dogs are poor climbers. I had no cord. If I had I would have dropped a noose over his head & hauled him up. But while I was thinking whether an available cord might be made out of clothing, he was looking keenly into the series of notched steps (49) & finger holds of the ice ladder I had made, as if counting them & fixing the position of each one of them in his mind. Then suddenly up he came with a nervy springy rush, hooking his paws into the notches & steps so quickly I could not see how it was done, whizzed past my head & screamed for joy. "Well done, Well done, little boy! Brave Boy!" I said, & tried to catch & caress him; but he would not be caught. Never before or since have I seen anything like so passionate a revulsion from fear to uncontrollable, triumphant joy. He flashed & darted hither & thither as if fairly demented, screaming & shouting, swirling round & round in giddy loops & circles like a leaf in a whirlwind, lying down & rolling over & over sidewise & head over heels, pouring forth a tumultuous flood of hysterical cries & sobs & gasping mutterings. [Then wildly yelling & screaming again.] And when I (50) ran up to him to shake him, fearing he might die of joy, he flashed off two or three hundred yards, his feet in a mist of motion; then turning suddenly he came back in wild rushes & launched himself at my face almost knocking me down, all the time screeching & screaming & shouting "Saved! Saved! Saved!" Then away again, dropping suddenly at times with his feet in the air, trembling & fairly sobbing. Such passionate emotion was enough to kill him. Moses' stately song of triumph after escaping the Egyptians & the Red Sea was nothing to it. Who could have guessed the capacity of the dull, enduring little fellow for all that most stirs this mortal frame. Nobody could have helped crying with him! But there is nothing like work for toning down either excessive fear or joy. So I ran ahead, calling him in as gruff a voice as I could command to come on & stop his nonsense, for we had far to go & it would (51) soon be dark.

Neither of us feared another trial like this. Heaven would surely count one enough for a lifetime. The ice ahead was gashed by thousands of crevasses but they were common ones. The joy of deliverance burned in us like fire, & we ran without fatigue, every muscle with immense rebound glorying in its strength. Stickeen flew across rather than jumped everything in his way, & not till dark did he settle into his normal fox-like gliding trot. At last the delectable mountains crowned with spruce came in sight, looming faintly in the gloaming, & soon we felt the sold rock beneath our feet, & were safe. Then came weariness. We stumbled down along the lateral moraine in the dark, over rocks & tree trunks, & through the bushes & devil-club thickets, & mossy logs & bowlders of the woods where we had sheltered in the morning, then out (52) on the level mud-slope of the terminal moraine. Danger had vanished & so had our strength. We reached camp about ten o'clock, & found a big fire & a big supper. A party of Hoona Indians had visited Mr. Young, bringing a gift of porpoise meat & wild strawberries, &

hunter Joe had brought in a wild goat. But we lay down too tired to eat much, & soon fell into a troubled sleep. The man who said, "The harder the toil the sweeter the rest," never was profoundly tired. Stickeen kept springing up & muttering in his sleep, no doubt dreaming he was still on the brink of the crevasse. So did I that night & many others long afterward when I was nervous & overtired.

After crossing that crevasse Stickeen was a changed dog. During the rest of the trip, instead of holding aloof, he would come to me at night when all was quiet around the campfire, & rest his head on my knee with a look of devotion as if I were his god. And oftentimes (53)[14] as he caught my eye he seemed to be trying to say "Wasn"t that an awful time we had together on the glacier?"

[Nothing in after years has dimmed that Alaska storm-day. As I write it all came rushing & roaring to mind as if I were again in the midst of it. Again I see the flying clouds with their rain-floods & snow, the ice-cliffs towering above the shrinking forest, the majestic ice-cascade, the vast glacier outspread before its white mountain fountains, & in the heart of it the tremendous crevasse—fit emblem of the valley of the shadow of death—low clouds trailing over it, the snow falling into it, & on its brink I see little Stickeen & I hear his cries for help & his shouts of joy. I have known many dogs, & many a story I could tell of their wisdom & devotion but to none do I owe so much as to Stickeen. (54)[15] At first the least knowable I suddenly knew him the best of all. By suffering he became transparent, & through him as through a window I have ever since been looking with clearer sympathy into all my animal neighbors.][16]

None of his old friends know what finally became of him. His fate is wrapped in mystery. When my work for the season was done I departed for California, & I never saw the

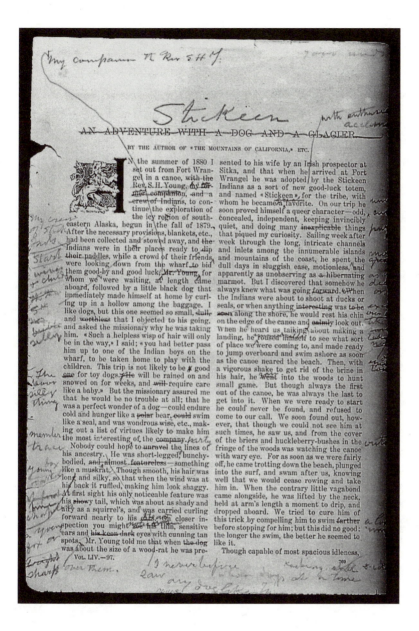

*The title page of the 1897 article published in* Century Magazine, *showing Muir's holographic revisions, including the restored original title.*

dear little fellow again. Mr. Young told me that in the summer of 1883 he was stolen by a tourist at Fort Wrangel & taken away on a steamer. If alive he is now nineteen years old. But he has probably left this world—crossed the last crevasse—& gone to another. But he will not be forgotten. [Come what may,] to me Stickeen is immortal.

—*John Muir*

# Endnotes

1.  This is the original 1897 title, which was changed by Robert Underwood Johnson to "An Adventure with a Dog and a Glacier."
2.  Page 2 from an earlier draft, 06470, in JMP (microfilm), 43/09374, pp. 1–2.
3.  From 06470, JMP (microfilm), 43/09374, p. 3.
4.  Ibid, pp. 5–6.
5.  Published in the 1909 edition.
6.  Published in the 1909 edition.
7.  From 06472, JMP (microfilm), 42/09029, p. 19.
8.  Ibid., p. 20.
9.  Published in the 1909 edition.
10. Published in the 1909 edition.
11. From 06472, JMP (microfilm), 42/09029, pp. 26, 30.
12. Ibid., p. 32.
13. Ibid., p. 34.
14. From 07876, JMP (microfilm), 43/09449, pp. 51–53 (as revised in 1908).
15. From 06472, JMP (microfilm), 42/09029, p. 54.
16. Published in the 1909 edition.

# The Later History of "Stickeen"

B y mid-June, 1897 Muir had completed the third and final draft, titled simply "Stickeen." A brusque letter to Johnson announced the results:

I have just finished that dog story & will send it in a day or two. The story easily told has been very hard to write. I think it is fairly well done. Please look it over, & if the magazine is going to be so crowded that it can not be published within say five or six months, then return it, as I'll be hanged rather than let you keep it as long as you have my last.[1]

The *Century* editor replied three weeks later. He was "correspondingly happy" with the piece, he explained, but some modifications were necessary. With editorial aplomb he said he had changed the title and had "done the story a service" by cutting away Muir's "digressions." Johnson was more interested in the effects on readers than in their edification. He didn't like the long description of the storm, and any hint that Stickeen was extraordinary until he faced the crevasse. "When you told this story," he said, "you simply said that this was a dog to whom you had paid very little attention before; but when in the manuscript you describe him at considerable length the reader is less prepared for the legitimate effect of his wonderful feat." To retain the element of surprise, Johnson "left out the reference to the previous crossings of the ice slivers, and treated it as if [the final crossing] . . . were the climax of the adventure." This, Johnson assured him, would capture the spirit of the oral version. "Remember that this is my story as well as yours," he continued. "I have heard it several times, and I know how it is most effective. Of course, I have not dared to add a line, and have only left out what seems to me extraneous matter."[2]

In short, Johnson had gutted the philosophical sections, reducing it to its original form as a thrilling adventure story. Surprisingly, given the amount of work he had done, Muir accepted the changes with good grace and even acknowledged Johnson's "part interest in the pup, as I would never have written the story had you not urged me to do so." But he disliked the stylistic emphasis:

> I hope however that in striving for artistic effect you will not blur the story. The narrative should I think be kept whole. Anyhow be sure to leave the legs of the article long enough to distinctly reach the ground. This Stickeen story easily told has cost me more time & work than anything else I ever wrote.[3]

Supremely self-confident, Johnson tried to stroke his author's wounded ego: "Do not be alarmed about the dog story. It is all right, and the country will say so when it is published."[4]

Johnson was right. Cutting away some of the descriptive incidentals and the philosophical "digressions" had improved it as an adventure story, and *Century* readers were delighted with the results. They had been entertained, and perhaps just a little educated. Muir had intended more edification, but bowed to the will of his editor.

The clamor for a book to follow-up the article demonstrated Stickeen's lasting appeal,[5] and Muir made plans to oblige with an expanded version.[6] Notes and clippings on dogs in the Muir papers show that he continued a pattern after 1897 that he had started in the early 1890s, as if the *Century* article were only an excerpt. But he was a prisoner of events beyond his control, events that in the next few years drew him further and further away from the adventure of 1880 and its philosophical significance.

In these later years he worked to keep alive the dog's memory, both to him and his family. In 1899 he came physically close to the scene of action nearly twenty years before. On his last trip to Alaska with the Harriman Expedition he stood on deck in silent vigil as the boat sailed past Taylor glacier.[7] About the same time he acquired a handsome collie for his frail daughter Helen, who suffered from respiratory illness. This was the new Stickeen, a family pet. Helen had to leave him behind when Muir took her to Arizona for her health in 1905. In 1908, after moving to Daggett in the Mojave Desert, she had the dog shipped to her; but he was too old, and the heat was too much. He died soon after.[8]

That same spring Muir revived the "canus" writing project. He was now alone in the Big House at Martinez. His wife had died in 1905, Wanda was married, and Helen still recuperating. The Hetch Hetchy fight had begun to heat up, but during a lull, he worked on a book draft of "Stickeen." Old complaints soon resurfaced. "Why even to dreamy wanderers should climbing Anglo-Saxon sentences be more difficult than climbing mountains?" he asked A. H. Sellers, a banker friend from Chicago.[9] But the pressure was on, both from his publisher, Houghton-Mifflin, and from Helen, who was anxious for her father to return to Daggett. The job was done in three months. To Helen he said he had rewritten and enlarged the story,[10] but that was

*Muir at Martinez with his family pet "Stikeen." Photograph by*
*Herbert W. Gleason, ca. 1901.*

misleading. Instead of reformulating and expanding it, he restored only a few lines of his first draft, tinkered a bit with the wording, and submitted to the publisher what was essentially the printed *Century* text. A letter to Helen summed up his attitude: he felt "sure it will be a good useful little booklet that will please you."[11] The "horizontal philosopher" had died with Muir's first draft of 1897.

Stickeen and other "fellow-creatures" continued to roam the margins of Muir's consciousness after 1909. He wanted to write another book bringing his thoughts on animals together, and even began compiling a few notes and aphorisms simply labeled "Animals."[12] But other priorities kept intruding. His eight-month trip to South America, then the last great fight over Hetch Hetchy, and finally the desperate effort to complete the book on Alaska, encroached on all other plans. His work pressed upon him to the end, but the dog's meaning, if not the memory, had dimmed. On his deathbed was an advanced draft of the Alaska book. In it he retold the dog story, relying mostly on his old journal notes of 1880 and the revisions he had made in the early 1890s.[13] The evolution of the story, the notes he had made in his library books, the drafts in which he had so carefully constructed a parable on the moral worth of animals—all were swept away. What was left was a simple descriptive narrative of his own struggle on the glacier. Stickeen had not faded entirely, but he was no longer the "herald of a new gospel." He was only a little dog, a faithful companion in good times and bad. If Muir never succeeded in converting the world to the new morality of animal egalitarianism, at least he had confirmed that dogs were more than man's best friend. He gave Stickeen—and by extension all so-called higher animals—an individual personality, a life worth living, an intrinsic value that today continues to gain recognition as the baseline of a broader ethic. Though nearly a century old, the story of "Stickeen" still offers fundamental lessons for humanity.

*Muir at his desk in the "scribble den" at Martinez, about 1892.*

# Endnotes

1. John Muir to RU Johnson, June 18, 1897, in *The John Muir Papers, 1858–1957*. Microform Edition. Ronald H. Limbaugh and Kirsten Lewis, eds. (Alexandria, VA: Chadwyck-Healey, Inc., 1986), 9/05551, hereafter JMP (microfilm).

2. RU Johnson to John Muir July 9, 1897, JMP (microfilm), 9/05576. Despite the disclaimer, Johnson did add words to the story—even a sentence or two—as his editorial marks and notes on the final draft prove. See "Stickeen" manuscript 07876, JMP (microfilm), 43/09449.

3. John Muir to RU Johnson, July 16, 1897, JMP (microfilm), 9/05581.

4. RU Johnson to John Muir, July 27, 1897, JMP (microfilm), 9/05584.

5. For example, see Julia M. Moores to Muir, October 11, 1897; E. G. Miller to Muir, January 24, 1898; in JMP (microfilm) 9/05637 & 10/05759.

6. John Muir to Helen Muir, June 4, 1908, in JMP (microfilm), 17/09783.

7. Edwin Way Teale reports this incident in *The Wilderness World of John Muir* (Boston: Houghton Mifflin, 1954), 277.

8. Helen Muir reminiscence, February 26, 1943, in JMP (microfilm) 51/00106.

9. Muir to A. H. Sellers, April 25, 1908, in JMP (microfilm), 17/09681.

10. Ferris Greenslet to Muir, April 9, 1908 (17/09648); Helen Muir to John Muir, June 11, 1908 (17/09791); Benjamin H. Ticknor to Muir, June 24, 1908 (17/09800); all in JMP (microfilm).

11. Muir to Helen, June 4, 1908, JMP (microfilm), 17/09783.

12. See John Muir, "Animals," (TCCMS, ca. 1910), in JMP (microfilm) 46/12082.

13. John Muir, *Travels in Alaska* (Boston and New York: Houghton Mifflin, c1915), 246–57.

# Notes on "Stickeen" in John Muir's Library

At least 105 of the 1,600 books that once formed part of John Muir's personal library contain evidence that Muir used the volume, directly or indirectly, in preparation of various "Stickeen" manuscripts. These books are listed below alphabetically by author in a standard bibliographic form. A sample of Muir's holographic remarks follows a brief annotation describing the extent of handwritten marks or notes. Where known, the date and source of acquisition are indicated. Three location codes are used: Holt-Atherton Library, University of the Pacific (UOPWA); Huntington Library, San Marino, California (HL); and Beinecke Library, Yale University (BL).

Bagehot, Walter. *Literary Studies. New Edition.* Edited, with a prefatory memoir, by Richard Holt Hutton. vol. 1. London: Longmans, Green, 1895. Three pages of Muir holographic endnotes, page index, draft text. Marginalia throughout volume. UOPWA.

    An English journalist and literary critic, Bagehot's best known work was *Physics and Politics* (1872), which does not appear in Muir's library inventory but which Muir may have read or at least heard about, since it enunciated a concept later known as "social Darwinism," which connected the idea of survival of the fittest with human social evolution.[1] Muir's marginal marks and endnotes in volume one of *Literary Studies* shows he was particularly interested in Bagehot's mysticism and his belief in immortality. In an essay on Hartley Coleridge, Bagehot wrote: "It is indeed a very overpowering thought, that we hold intercourse with creatures who are as much strangers to us, as mysterious as if they were the fabulous, unearthly beings, more powerful than man, and yet his slaves, which Eastern superstitions have invented." Muir responded with a series of thoughts on Stickeen: "I have oftentimes regretted the dumbness of animals/ Their inability to speak up & tell their own story . . . In times of deadly peril fortitude of common kind however brave is replaced by deep hidden power with wh we seem to have nothing to do/ . . . began to see there was something in him & more & more regretted it was all unspeakable/ . . . to understand him seemed like chasing will-o-the-wisps profoundly stoical."

————. *Literary Studies. New Edition.* Edited, with a prefatory memoir, by Richard Holt Hutton. vol. 2. London: Longmans, Green, 1895. 2 pp. holographic index, notes, draft text. UOPWA.

On page 13 of the text Muir marks a quotation from Shakespeare's "Henry V" on love of danger by nobility, and a subsequent comment by Bagehot: "We see these men setting forth or assembling to defend their King and Church; and we see it without surprise; a rich daring loves danger; a deep excitability likes excitement. If we look around us, we may see what is analogous." Muir's endnote comment: "Ex[cellent] Can[us] 13 Had he not seemed so dull one might guess he loved danger."

————. *Literary Studies (Miscellaneous Essays). New Series.* Edited, with a prefatory memoir, by Richard Holt Hutton. vol. 3. London: Longmans Green, 1895. 3 pp. holographic index, notes, draft text. UOPWA.

Muir liked Bagehot's commentary on late eighteenth century English life: "Like most comfortable people, those of that time possessed a sleepy, supine sagacity." The endnote transformed it to a characterization of Stickeen: "Can ex . . . possessed a sleepy uncomplaining sagacity J. M./ Intellect so slow & sleepy of movement as to raise doubts as to whether he possessed any at all worth the name." After more reading Muir came back to the same theme and wrote: "He seemed at first sight to possess all the tranquil advantages of dullness & ignorance . . . Had a dull sleepy sagacity . . . and as he lay comfortably by the camp fire with his watching eyes ever on duty I thought again & again I wish you could write."

In this volume Muir also marked Bagehot's quotation of a response to a flippant remark by Sydney Smith after the death of Henry Crabb Robinson. "But how could you," said the indignant respondent, "expect their 'remains' to be made fun of?" That triggered another idea about the dog that Muir recorded in the endnote: "Wholly incapable of making fun never tired/ a character—nothing odd picturesque, grotesque—too smooth & small featureless for that."

Bayne, Peter. *Lessons From My Masters, Carlyle, Tennyson and Ruskin.* New York: Harper & Bro., 1879. 2 pp. holographic notes. HL.

In this series of essays by a popular nineteenth-century biographer, Muir took note of the author's remarks on the erratic fortunes of men of letters. "Such men are the flower of this lower world," said Bayne. Muir marked the passage and wrote: "the bright affectionate flrs of doghood/ . . . Stick a weed, uncertain ancest/ Looking at a boulder hard to realize the mad enthusiastic whirling dancing rolling action it is capable of & so no one might guess the action potential of wh Stick was capable."

Blackie, John Stuart. *On Self-Culture, Intellectual, Physical, and Moral: A Vade Mecum for Young Men and Students.* New York: Chas. Scribner's Sons [ca. 1895]. 3 pp. holographic notes, page index. HL.

In a chapter on "Physical Culture," the author, describing the partaking of a hearty meal, quoted Chancellor Thurlow: "*totus in illis,* 'a whole man to one thing at one time.'" Muir underlined the passage and wrote in an endnote: "Can) A whole man to one thing at one time / never could there be a more desperate life & death concentration of a whole being on one thing, all the world beside shut out."

Brown, John. *Horae Subsecivae.* New ed. in 3 vols.; 1st series. Edinburgh: David Douglas, 1889. Inscribed inside fly leaf: "Wm Keith SF 91." JM holographic inscription follows: "John Muir Martinez 92" 6 pp. holographic index, endnotes, draft text. UOPWA.

Muir's extensive endnotes in the volumes of Brown are discussed in chapter four above. Among the numerous one-line characterizations of dogs on the back pages of this volume is a colorful ecological thought inspired by reflecting on what might have happened had the ice bridge failed: "What poor bits of white clean ice-pinched skeletons we would make after being pinched in the tremendous press of the gl for a century or

2 & then cast upon the terminal moraine & adorned with epilobiums & sedges."

Brown, John. *Horae Subsecivae*. New ed. in 3 vols.; 2nd series. Edinburgh: David Douglas, 1889. Gift of William Keith. 4 pp. holographic JM topical index, notes, commentary, draft text. UOPWA.

   Brown's description of Toby, a dog "not ugly enough to be interesting," gave Muir an idea for "Stickeen." Toby, said the *Horae* author, "was of the bull-terrier variety, coarsened through much mongrelism and a dubious and varied ancestry." Said Muir in the corresponding endnote: "There was not enough [of Stickeen] . . .to be interesting/ Inherited from many generations of downtrodden fathers & mothers in the interior of Alaska." He also made note of Brown's reaction to the fate of Puck, a street dog scheduled for death after his capture by police: "In ten minutes he would have been in the next world; for I am one of those who believe dogs *have* a next world, and why not?"

Browne, Sir Thomas. *Religio Medici and Urn-burial*. London: J. M. Dent, 1896. $^3/_4$ p. holographic notes. HL.

   "Stickeen" was nearing final draft stage when Muir read this edition of Browne's remarkable essay written nearly 350 years before. He underscored with a flourish Browne's chapter heading, "All Flesh is Grass"— the same motto Muir had read in his Bible as a boy and had used to inscribe the pendulum of a clock he had constructed in the basement of the farmhouse at Hickory Hill.[2] In the chapter Browne had written a sobering commentary on the facts of human existence: "we are what we all abhor, *Anthropophagi* and Cannibals, devourers not onely of men, but of our selves; and that not in an allegory, but a positive truth." Muir's endnote remarks looked on the brighter side of nature's life and death cycle: "Ex Can Rocks with entombed animals all alike falling in beauty to ashes making wreaths of embroidery like mouldings beauty from beauty, beauty on beauty."

Carlyle, Thomas. *Critical and Miscellaneous Essays: Collected and Republished*. vol. 1. London: Chapman & Hall, [1869?]. 3 pp. holographic topical index, notes, comments, draft text. UOPWA.

   Carlyle's—and Muir's—debt to Shakespeare, seen in this volume, is noted in chapter four. In another note not related to the text, Muir said

Stickeen "had none of that kittinish drollery so common in small dogs/ No enthusiasm of character unsprightly/ among all his natural gifts calm endurance the most noticeable."

————. *Critical and Miscellaneous Essays: Collected and Republished*. vol. 2. London: Chapman & Hall, [1869?]. 5 pp. holographic topical index, notes, comments, draft text. UOPWA.

The essay on Burns was one of Muir's favorites in this volume. In addition to the clock metaphor discussed in chapter three, Muir found particularly relevant the description of Burns' love of all things and his "mysterious brotherhood" with nature. It seemed a way to summarize his "ice work" with Stickeen: "I felt happy & rich that day & g[o]t nobly compensated for all the dreadful nerve-drawing danger in getting closer . . . into the mysterious brotherhood of all gods creatures."

————. *Critical and Miscellaneous Essays: Collected and Republished*. vol. 3. London: Chapman & Hall, [1869]. 4 end pages index, notes, comments. UOPWA.

Muir's reading of this volume spurred the development of another metaphor, the "window . . . into infinitude" described in chapter three. He also appreciated Carlyle's transcription of the "Song of the Alps," a lyrical poem by Friedrich Schiller. The first few stanzas bear remarkable similarity to both the imagery and language of "Stickeen": "By the edge of the chasm is a slippery Track,/ The torrent beneath, and the mist hanging o'er thee; / The cliffs of the mountain, huge, rugged and black,/ Are frowning like giants before thee:/ And, wouldst thou not waken the sleeping Lawine,/ Walk silent and soft through the deadly ravine./ That Bridge, with its dizzying perilous span,/ Aloft o'er the gulf and its flood suspended,/ Think'st thou it was built by the art of man,/ By his hand that grim old arch was bended?/ Far down in the jaws of the gloomy abyss/ The water is boiling and hissing,—forever will hiss."

————. *Critical and Miscellaneous Essays: Collected and Republished*. vol. 4. London: Chapman & Hall, [1869?]. 4 pp. holographic topical index, notes, draft text. UOPWA.

An essay on Goethe in this volume reinforced Muir's vision of the oneness of creation. He marked Carlyle's quotation of Teufelsdröck on the divinity and mystical oneness of humanity, and wrote on a back page: "It should be interesting that the maker of men is also the maker of d[og]s & put into them a lit[tle] of everything that went to the making of men."

———. *The French Revolution: a History.* vol. 1. London: Chapman & Hall, [1837, later ed.?]. 3 pp. holographic topical index, notes, draft text. UOPWA.

Muir read this volume thoroughly, but apparently not until after he had completed the final draft of "Stickeen." When working on the manuscript he used this book simply as note paper. Nevertheless the endnote is poignant: "(Canis) Sobs & suplications moans & groans as if some grand nation were going to ruin poor fellow his tongue was loose now—a perfect f[oun]t[ai]n of sighs & tears—boiled & swelled as he saught deliverance from the awful gulf."

———. *The French Revolution.* vol. 3. London: Chapman & Hall [1837]. 1 p. holographic index, notes. UOPWA.

Not a significant volume in the "Stickeen" story, but still worth noting because of Muir's alliterative endnote which seems to have no connection to Carlyle's text: "(Canis) lashed into a foam & fury of fear."

———. *History of Friedrich II. of Prussia, called Frederick the Great.* vol. 1. London: Chapman & Hall, n.d. $1/2$ p. holographic topical index, draft text. UOPWA.

Carlyle wrote that Wolfgang Wilhelm, ancestor of Frederick, was "evidently very high and stiff in his ways" in proposing a marriage designed to add territory to the Prussian elector's holdings. Muir changed the context and used the same wording, with slight modification: "(Canis) Very high & stiff in {his ways} manners wh[ich] well became his silence but not at all his short legs, & now his silence gave way & he wailed aloud his (woeful) fears."

———. *History of Friedrich II of Prussia, Called Frederick the Great.* vol. 2. London: Chapman & Hall, n.d. 2 pp. holographic topical index, draft text. UOPWA.

Muir admired Carlyle's epistemology, as expressed in a description in this volume of the young Frederick's response to an enlightened French tutor. His mind was stimulated, said Carlyle, "to a lively, and in some sort genial, perception of things round him;—of the strange confusedly opulent Universe he had got into; and of the noble and supreme function which Intelligence holds there; supreme, in Art as in Nature, beyond all other functions whatsoever." He was also amused by Carlyle's story of a royal dinner debauch in which "a new miracle appears on the field: the largest Cake ever baked by the Sons of Adam." Here was another image for Stickeen—a "comically small indirect son of Adam," he wrote in the endnote.

————. *History of Friedrich II of Prussia, called Frederick the Great.* vol. 4. London: Chapman & Hall, n.d.] 1 p. holographic draft text. UOPWA.

Using the back pages for draft paper Muir reformulated a familiar theme, the unity of creation. "I cannot tell here," he wrote, "how much this day on the Alaska ice did for me in definably & surely widening my view of the world & all its peoples 2 footed & 4 footed/ I saw them & believed & felt sure that all the creatures of God on earth are one, that the sun & the moon rose & shone & the stars for all of us alike—not simply as a speculative romantic guess or belief but really in very fact."

————. *History of Friedrich II of Prussia, called Frederick the Great.* vol. 5. London: Chapman & Hall, n.d. $^1/_4$ p. holographic draft text & page references. UOPWA.

"The gods had not been kind to Stickeen {him} in size & feature," wrote Muir in a brief and disconnected endnote. It must have been drafted in 1897, since before that time Muir referred to the dog by the older spelling, "Stickine."

————. *History of Friedrich II of Prussia, called Frederick the Great.* vol. 6. London: Chapman & Hall, n.d. $^1/_2$ p. holographic draft text. UOPWA.

As is clear from two separate sets of holographic markings on the back pages of this volume, Muir wrote the "Stickeen" notes before reading the text. His endnote reiterates a theme he had explored on the back pages of other volumes of Carlyle. "Of all the dogs walking {trotting} the earth this day of 1880," he recorded, "only Stikin[e] was real to me & how clear piercing unforgettable it all was & how widely the gates were thrown ajar that separate men & animals."

————. *History of Friedrich II of Prussia, called Frederick the Great.* vol. 7. London: Chapman & Hall, n.d. 1 p. holographic index, notes, draft text. UOPWA.

From Carlyle's description of Frederick's determination during his army's midnight march toward Silesia, Muir conjured up a picture of Stickeen, "gazing hushed & meditative in life & death concentration" at the bridge. His mind "declared the thing impossible in a dog nature," but as the dog approached the trial Muir turned to prayer: "poor lit[tle] boy. Now some angel help him hold these 4 small feet that they may not slip."

———. *History of Friedrick II. of Prussia, called Frederick the Great.* vol. 8. London: Chapman & Hall, n.d. 1 topical index note; 1 text draft. UOPWA.

Muir's only note in this book was a single detached phrase: "(Canis) Never in the least gay, frolicsome (anguish)."

———. *Latter-day Pamphlets.* London: Chapman & Hall, [1850]. 2 pp. holographic index, notes. UOPWA.

From Carlyle's discussion of the qualities of a stump speaker, Muir generated this observation on "Stickeen": "Excellent silence a much rarer & more difficult gift than excellent speech/ A poor little dumb child dog of the Alaskan wilderness."

———. *The Life of John Sterling.* London: Chapman & Hall, [1851] 1870. 2 pp. holographic topical index, notes. UOPWA.

Separate pencil markings in this book indicate that Muir's first reading occured before he began to draft the "Stickeen" manuscript. From a letter Sterling wrote Carlyle in 1835, Muir extracted two phrases he recorded on the back pages: "The sense of a oneness of life & destiny in all existence/ Boundless exuberance of beauty & power around us." Reviewing these notes later, he inserted at the left margin the word "Canis." The concepts, if not the exact phraseology, appear in the final draft of "Stickeen."

———. *Oliver Cromwell's Letters and Speeches: with Elucidations.* vol. 1. London: Chapman & Hall, n.d. $1/2$ p. holographic topical index, draft text. UOPWA.

Describing Cromwell's hypochondria, Carlyle wrote: "Let Oliver take comfort in his dark sorrows and melancholies. The quantity of sorrow he has, does it not mean withal the quantity of *sympathy* he has, the quantity of faculty and victory he shall yet have? Our sorrow is the inverted image of our nobleness. The depth of our despair measures what capability and height of claim we have to hope. Black smoke as of Tophet filling all your universe, it can yet by true heart-energy become *flame*, and brilliancy of Heaven. Courage!" From this passage Muir derived an endnote summary of Stickeen's experience: "The brave thing was done & he was happy/ where now his torper & silence-roused/ The depth of his despair was now measured & manifested by his joy What a sunburst of joy at deliverance from the jaws of Death."

————. *Oliver Cromwell's Letters and Speeches: with Elucidations.* vol. 2. London: Chapman & Hall, n.d. $1/4$ p. holographic notes. UOPWA.

The back page records only a disjointed endnote not connected to the text: "(Can)/ Ran about shrieking distracted/ Hysterical fury of joy/ one vast sheet of gashed wrinkled desolation."

————. *Oliver Cromwell's Letters and Speeches: with Elucidations.* vol. 3. London: Chapman & Hall, n.d. 2 pp. holographic topical index, draft text. UOPWA.

In this flowing and evocative endnote, apparently not abstracted from the text, Muir focused on the majesty and power of the storm: "(Can) 4 inches wide but swung across as wide & deep a chasm seemed narrow as a rope/ On the day of his weakness was the day of his power {his power & strength of mind}/ . . . The tempest was abroad lashing the dreary land but nothing bodeful in its roar to me—often heard,—but strange Stick should face it—The woods moan & howl in the heavy salt-blast from the sea & its roar blends with the roar of many a torrent swollen from the rain falling in cascades showery gray thru the gloomy clds & rain/ He accepted favors with a slow heavy or dull satisfaction/ Blue abysses beautiful & vivid as the jagged lightning of a black storm & as terrible/ a grand day fairly stupid & intoxicated with the sport of the Lord/ God was abroad that day in bodily form riding on the wings of the wind . . . A day that made rocks & streams dance into forms of beauty into beautiful fruitful life-giving landscapes."

————. *Oliver Cromwell's Letters and Speeches: with Elucidations.* vol. 4. London: Chapman & Hall, n.d. 1 p. holographic topical index, draft text. UOPWA.

Another free-flowing endnote, detached from Carlyle's text, in which Muir returns to the oneness theme. Some of the these characterizations he

incorporated into the final draft: "(Can) a dog of gentle blood—the image
of god very obscure in him/ Overawed . . . Kept silence whether noble &
proud or only stupid hard to tell . . . [after 83] Animals are strangely apart
from us/ Wild people know them best. This brought me nearer than all my
other meetings—they fear & rejoice like us."

————. *Oliver Cromwell's Letters and Speeches: with Elucidations.* vol. 5.
London: Chapman & Hall, n.d. $^1/_4$ p. holographic page references; 1 p.
draft text. UOPWA.

Using the end leaves of the book as draft paper, Muir worked out an
extended description of the storm they faced on the day of the adventure:
"The wind came laden with the brine of the broad Pacific Ocean trashing
the forests & wandering far over the icy plane of the gls gurgling & moaning in chasms & hollows of blue ice & surging against a thousand mtns.
with rain & snow on its wings but the forests & mtns & crystal gls have
felt & heard the like before a 1000 times & seems to like this noble sea-
blast/ Came to another opening mouth of the gl wh I fancied discharging
into the Ocean 1000s of sharp blades 50 & 100 ft high leaning forward
one behind the other in unvaried succession like the wild updashing flame-
shaped waves of a tremendous cataract torn & tossed in a jagged rock
channel."

A humorous colloquialism also appears in this endnote. Muir worked
it into the final draft, but it was blue-penciled by the editor: "as he bounded
effortlessly over crevasses that brought one to a cautious halt often thought
of a Scotch proverb Ye canna tell by the looks of a toad how far he can
jump."

————. *Tales by Musaeus, Tieck, Richter. Translated from the German by Thomas Carlyle.* London: Chapman & Hall; New York: Scribner, Welford,
[1827] 1871. 4 pp. holographic topical index, notes, comments, draft text.
UOPWA.

Another series of fragmentary endnotes not connected to Carlyle's
text. Here Muir returns to the task of deciphering the dog's complex character: "(Canis) Begging eyes/ had a tough compact stunted look like a tree
growing on the extreme border of Arctic forest/ . . . He had {felt} none of
the black-gray forebodings that threatened me. his little feet twinkled in a
sober workaday confidence over the ice like those of an Esquimos sledge
team/ Baleful sounds in crevasses & the wind, was shaken in a whirl of

bitter tumultous fear becoming evermore bitter as he ran along the brink of the gulf/ He followed -couldnt get rid of him as well might the earth shake off the moon/ I had led his master into trouble now his humble comp[anion]—when alone none to help but also by way of compensation none to hinder—/Begged with all his body eloquently to be allowed to go—/ not shamefaced but shamebodied."

Chamberlin, Joseph Edgar. *The Listener in the Country.* vol. 2. Boston: Copeland & Day, 1896. $^1/_2$ p. holographic index, notes, one draft sentence on "Stickeen."

Muir worked on a different version of his "window" metaphor on the back pages of this book. (cf. chapter three.)

Coleridge, Samuel Taylor. *Biographia Literaria; or, Biographical Sketches of My Literary Life and Opinions; and Two Lay Sermons.* London: George Bell & Sons, 1889. Front flyleaf inscription: "Wm Keith / Berkeley" 2 pp. endnotes; margin lines intermittent throughout text. HL.

Muir jotted down notes on "Stickeen" on the back pages, then later returned for a careful reading of the text. Stickeen "had the air of a surely disciplined dog of old experience like people who make themselves stupid to everybody but themselves who by slow steady thinking no tricks or accomplishments either of the parlor or kennel/ Scoldings & caresses were the same to him/ The trees on the cliffs lending from the sea blast/ Sublime love of ds for their masters & strength of feeling: but I was not his master & why he insisted on following me I dont know; Nothing so quickly brings sympathy as fear of death."

———. *Lectures and Notes on Shakespeare, and other English Poets.* London: George Bell and Sons, 1888. 2 pp. holographic notes. Flyleaf inscription: "Wm. Keith." HL.

In his endnote Muir makes use of an anecdote by Coleridge to avouch the intellectual capacity of the dog. Coleridge said Bishop Jeremy Taylor once described a great man as "naturally a coward, as indeed most men are, knowing the value of life, but the power of his reason enabled him, when required, to conduct himself with uniform courage and hardihood. The good bishop, perhaps, had in his mind a story, told by one of the ancients, of a Philosopher and a Coxcomb, on board the same ship during a storm: the Coxcomb reviled the Philosopher for betraying marks of fear:

'Why are you so frightened? I am not afraid of being drowned: I do not care a farthing for my life.'—'You are perfectly right,' said the Philosopher, 'for your life is not worth a farthing.'" Muir's endnote: Stickeen "plainly & reasonably dreaded losing life as if like a philosopher he knew the value of it/ He was gifted with the faculties of hope & fear—fellow-mortals."

————. *Miscellanies, Aesthetic and Literary: to Which is Added the Theory of Life*. London: George Bell and Sons, 1888. Inside flyleaf inscription: "Wm. Keith." 2 pp. holographic page index, notes. HL.

A passage from an essay on pedantry provides supporting evidence for Muir's belief that the dog's actions were not merely instinctive. "The rough sheep-dog," wrote Coleridge, "is almost indispensable to the civilization of the human race. He appears to possess not valuableness only, but even worth! His various moral qualities, which seem above the effects of mere instinct devoid of will, compel our respect and regard, and excite our gratitude to him, as well as for him. Yet neither his paramount utility, no, nor even his incorruptible fidelity and disinterested affection, enable us to equal him, in outward beauty, with the cruel and cowardly panther, or leopard, or tiger, the hate and horror of the flock and of the shepherd." Muir's endnote jottings reiterate the point he develops in later drafts: "Can) stoical complacency/ . . . The d[og]s moral qualities etc above instincts/ The operations of his intellect seen only in slyly watching the movements about the camp etc."

————. *The Poetical Works of Samuel Taylor Coleridge*. Ed. with introduction and notes by T. Ashe. 2 v. [v. 2 missing]. London: George Bell and Sons, 1885. Inside front flyleaf inscribed: "Wm. Keith S. F." 1 pp. holographic notes, draft text. HL.

Though marginal marks and endnotes show that Muir's reading was thorough, Coleridge provided a mood rather than specific content for the "Stickeen" manuscript. Near the end of "Honour" on page 133, for example, is this couplet: "A hideous hag the Enchantress Pleasure seems, / And all her joys appear but feverous dreams." Muir recorded a terse endnote: "133 (Intro)/ pleasurable exultation (Can)/ desperate energy of misery." Earlier on the same back page he spoke of seeing in the dog a "gleam of a subtle keenness from his eyes now & then when anything out of the common was going on that piqued curiosity—to be succeeded by days of blank expressionless dullness."

————. *The Table Talk and Omniana of Samuel Taylor Coleridge.* Arranged and ed. by T. Ashe. London: George Bell and Sons, 1888. 3 pp. holographic endnotes. HL.

The extensive endnotes, and the use of the original spelling, "Stickine," demonstrate that Muir used this book very early in the development of his narrative. As mentioned in chapter four, Muir's use of the "chain of being" in "Stickeen" comes from Coleridge's journal entry of July 9, 1827: "In the very lowest link in the vast and mysterious chain of Being, there is an effort, although scarcely apparent, at individualisation; but it is almost lost in the mere separate, but subordinate to anything in man. At length, the animal rises to be on a par with the lowest power of the human nature."

Muir also took an idea from this book to develop the notion of Stickeen's ability to communicate. His endnote explains: "Brute animals says Coleridge have the vowel sounds only man the consonants/ But Stickine uttered his woe on all the human language—at least so it seemed to me."

On the matter of animal souls, Coleridge was influenced by Cartesian logic, as the following entry, marked by Muir, clearly demonstrates: "Either we have an immortal soul, or we have not. If we have not, we are beasts; the first and wisest of beasts, it may be; but still true beasts. We shall only differ in degree, and not in kind; just as the elephant differs from the slug. But by the concession of all the materialists of all the schools, or almost all, we are not of the same kind as beasts—and this also we say from our own consciousness. Therefore, methinks, it must be the possession of a soul within us that makes the difference." Muir, though at odds with Coleridge on this issue, did not bother to dispute the position in the endnotes.

Crabbe, George. *The Poetical Works of George Crabbe.* London: Gall and Inglis, n.d. 1 p. holographic topical index, notes. UOPWA.

Muir thought a stanza from Letter X of Crabbe's "The Borough" an "excellent" depiction of some of his own thoughts when confronting the icy crevasse. He marked the passage where the poet described an elder man approaching death, after the doctor has given up and the last prayer uttered: "Here all the aid of man to man must end,/ Here mounts the soul to her eternal Friend:/ The tenderest love must here its tie resign, /And give th' aspiring heart to love divine."

Dante Alighieri, *The Divine Comedy; or, Vision of Hell, Purgatory and Paradise.* Translated by the Rev. Henry Francis Cary. New York: A. L. Burt, [189–?]. 2 pp. holographic notes; draft text. HL.

The term "Canis," inserted in the margins of his endnotes, indicates that Muir read the epic poem before working on his own story, then went back over both notes and text for ideas. As allegory the poem has close parallels to Muir's perception of his own experiences. That Dante's vivid image of hell influenced Muir's descriptions of both the storm and the deep crevasse confronting man and dog on the Taylor glacier can be seen by comparing the text of Muir's final draft in chapter five with the follow-ing passages, most of which Muir marked in the text: "It were no easy task, how savage wild/ That forest, how robust and rough its growth. . . . He me encouraged. 'Be thou stout: be bold./ Down such a steep flight must we now descend. . . . But that the wind, arising to my face,/ Breathes on me from below. Now on our right/ I heard the cataract beneath us leap/ With hideous crash; whence bending down to explore,/ New terror I con-ceived at the steep plunge. . . . So that, all trembling, close I crouch'd my limbs,/ And then distinguish'd, unperceived before,/ By the dread torments that on every side/ Drew nearer, how our downward course we wound. . . . Unwonted joy renew'd, soon as I 'scaped/ Forth from the atmosphere of deadly gloom."

Eliot, George. *Wit and Wisdom.* 1885. 4–5 pp. holographic index, notes, draft text. UOPWA.

Muir read this anthology carefully and was influenced by specific pas-sages, especially Eliot's affection for the "lower animals": "I have all my life had a sympathy for mongrel ungainly dogs, who are nobody's pets; and I would rather surprise one of them by a pat and a pleasant morsel, than meet the condescending advances of the loveliest Skye-terrier who has his cushion by my lady's chair." Elsewhere she writes: "Poor dog! I've a strange feeling about the dumb [68] things as if they wanted to speak, and it was a trouble to 'em because they couldn't. I can't help being sorry for the dogs always, though perhaps there's no need. But they may well have more in them than they know how to make us understand, for we can't say half what we feel, with all our words." Muir responded in an endnote: "We are in the habit of thinking that the higher nature can never fail to understand the lower, while comprehending the lower, but this is far from being true/ man is strangely separate from the lower animals."

Eliot's remarks on the power of two souls uniting inspired Muir's symbolic linking with the soul of Stickeen. She wrote: "Blessed influence of one true loving human soul on another! . . . sometimes [ideas] . . . are made flesh . . . they are clothed in a living human soul, with all its conflicts, its faith, and its love. Then their presence is a power, then they shake us like a passion, and we are drawn after them with gentle compulsion, as flame is drawn to flame."

Muir's endnote extrapolation: "Under the stress of this supreme trial Stickine became a living human soul/ flesh of my flesh bone of my bone/ . . . in this life & death struggle, fancied I could see & hear his distressed heart beats/ to say that I sympathized with him would not tell the true story, If felt & heard his heartbeats It required no more discernment to read every motion, for [h]is soul was bare & my vision was sharp with the clearing pains of my own deliverance, for I had just passed through the fire/ My heart was caught by its own deadly struggle/ as if all the accumulated riches of his life arose to view in one grand display like a tree on fire giving out all the century gains from the sun in one blaze of fire."

Emerson, Ralph W. *The Prose Works of Ralph Waldo Emerson.* New and Revised Ed. In Two Volumes. vol. 1. Boston: Fields, Osgood & Co., 1870. 6 pp. holographic holographic index, notes on back pages. Muir's holographicic marks throughout text. BL.

The elaborate marginalia and endnotes provide ample evidence of Muir's thorough scrutiny of this work sent him by the author in 1871. Long after his first reading of the work, Muir returned to it while "Stickeen" was in draft stage, finding numerous passages relevant to the perception of the dog as transcendental messenger, a symbol of spiritual unity with all creation. Through Emerson, said Muir, he gained "a nearer clearer sympathy with fellow creatures. . . . The spirit of Stickine made all the landscape brighter for me—a 4 footed man." Elsewhere, his mind on the crevasse, Muir marked a "C" beside a sobering thought inspired by a reading of Emerson's "Nature": "What good had nature forms in us, she pardons no mistakes."

Goethe. *Wilhelm Meister's Apprenticeship and Travels. Translated from the German of Goethe by Thomas Carlyle.* vol. 1. London: Chapman & Hall, n.d. 4 pp. holographic topical index, notes, comments, draft text. UOPWA.

Carlyle's introduction, addressing the role of translator, provides Muir with a telling phrase for "Stickeen." Wrote Carlyle: "A genuine seer and speaker, under what conditions soever, shall be welcome to us: has not he seen [ital omitted] somewhat, of great Nature our common Mother's bringing-forth; seen it, loved it, laid his heart open to it and to the Mother of it, so that he can now rationally speak it for Us?" Wrote Muir in the endnote: "(Canis) a babychild of our common mother/ his heart & mind laid open." Later on in early drafts of the manuscript he tried to bring this line together with his "clock" metaphor, but abandoned it before the final draft.

Other notes on "Stickeen" fill the back pages, but some were erased for reasons unknown. Most are short iterations, disconnected to Carlyle's text.

———. *Wilhelm Meister's Apprenticeship and Travels*. Thomas Carlyle, Translator. vol. 2. London: Chapman & Hall, [1824]. 2 $1/_2$ pp. holographic index, notes. UOPWA.

Muir empathized with Goethe's description of a mountain climb in which the climber, after reaching "the topmost summit," could peer "down from it into the horrid depth" and "see furious mountain-torrents foaming through black abysses." It was another version of the crevasse, but Muir's endnote lightened the imagery: "Ex) (Canis) Immeasurable gulf has life wh grandest work of art has not." In a second set of notes on the back pages he developed an independent thought: "Canis/ Every now & then a knowing turn of the eyes suggested that this seeming dullness might be the dignified reserve & seering [?] of some little prince dog in disguise & therefore I was stimulated to watch him as a curious problem / A free independent yet friendly & law-abiding vegabond [sic] owning nothing in commercial sense yet possessing all the world."

Goldsmith, Oliver. *Poems, Plays and Essays*. New York: T. Y. Crowell, n.d. 2 pp. holographic index on back pages; notes; numerous margin lines in text. UOPWA.

In an essay on "Mad Dogs," the author wrote: "Of all the beasts that graze the lawn, or hunt the forest, a dog is the only animal, that leaving his fellows, attempts to cultivate the friendship of man. . . . How unkind then to torture this faithful creature, who has left the forest to claim the protection of man! How ungrateful a return to the trusty animal for all its services." Muir carried that theme into the endnotes: "(Can Ex) The only animal that without reason casts its lot with man—& makes him his god with a fidelity & submission under all conditions that puts the perpendicular animal of wisdom to shame/ dogged inspired equanimity/ . . . If in thus holding up the deadly distress & afterjoy of this lit. d. I have brought my readers nearer to animals the vast family of our poor earth born companions & fellow mortals then the telling of my little story will not be in vain." After warning himself against too much moralizing, Muir recorded another lesson: "In spite of nerve & power of will we are all frail incapable of directing our steps away from danger & ignorant always of knowing what is to happen in our little walks thru life/ This truth is illustrated by the smoothist & levelist of human lives & no doubt by the lives of the smallest animals if we could only see them (get near enough to see them)." Fortunately he found better ways to express these thoughts in later drafts.

Gowing, Lionel Francis. *Five Thousand Miles in a Sledge: A Mid-winter Journey Across Siberia.* New York: D. Appleton, 1890. Inscribed inside front flyleaf: "Wm. Keith." 2 notes. HL.

Though none of Muir's standard codes for "Stickeen" indicated, the content of the short note on a back page is sufficient to link it to the dog story: "Gentle placidity, endowed with imperturbable equanimity." In the final draft Muir said the dog's "equanimity was so immovable it seemed due to unfeeling ignorance."

Green, John Richard. *Letters of John Richard Green.* Leslie Stephen. New York: Macmillan, 1901. 5 pp. holographic index, notes, draft ms. UOPWA.

After the first published version of "Stickeen" appeared in 1897, Muir continued to find passages he related to the story, as his notes in this book indicate. Green, a widely-read British historian, was troubled by the implications of Darwin. A letter he wrote in 1863 gave Muir another perspective on the implications of "Stickeen": "If Man," wrote Green, "seem but an outcome of the advance of the animal world, 'a monkey with something non-monkey about him,' what if Science confirms the Apostle's grand hint of the unity of the world about us with our spiritual selves, 'the whole creation groaneth and travaileth in bondage,' etc.? If there are hints of a purpose to be wrought out in them as it has been wrought out in us? Well, it is a grand thought—little more as yet—but one which may widen for us our conception of the revelation in Christ—the revelation of God's love to His children. . . . Is He the Father of man only, is He not the 'All-fader' as our old Teuton fathers called him, is He not the Father of the Brute also?" Muir indexed the passage as "Animals & Men" in the endnote, then afterward—perhaps in 1908 when he was working on the book *Stickeen*—wrote "Stick" beside his note.

Hawthorne, Nathaniel. *A Wonder Book, Tanglewood Tales, and Grandfather's Chair.* vol. 1. Boston: Houghton Mifflin, 1884. $3/4$ p. holographic index, notes, draft text. UOPWA.

From Hawthorne's story "The Pygmies," describing the titanic struggle between Antaeus and Hercules, Muir crafted a metaphor designed for "Stickeen" but cut before the final draft: "Canis) He looked pathetically weak & small in the uproar & obscurity of the tempest/ Like Antaeus every time we touch the mtns we are stronger."

————. *The Blithedale Romance.* Boston: Houghton Mifflin, 1884. 3 pp. holographic index, notes, draft text. UOPWA.

Among the extensive endnotes on the back pages, only one appears to have been inspired directly from the printed text. Referring to the character of women, Hawthorne wrote: "They are not natural reformers, but become such by the pressure of exceptional misfortune." Muir's endnote corollary: "We never know until tried what is in us. In stress of mortal danger in our own or others behalf we do what under other calm common moods appear utterly impossible. & therefore tried souls always wonder more at themselves than at others." His observation never reached the final draft of "Stickeen"; nevertheless, the message was implicit.

————. *The Dolliver Romance and Fanshawe.* Boston: Houghton, Mifflin, 1884. $1/2$ pp. holographic notes, 2 index entries, most draft text erased. UOPWA.

In several short endnotes, Muir sketched out a few thoughts he later erased. Only one is connected to Hawthorne's text. Contrasting the infirmities of the elderly Dr. Dolliver with the freshness of youth, Hawthorne wrote: "the ashes of many perishable things have fallen upon our youthful fire, but beneath them lurk the seeds of inextinguishable flame. So powerful is this instinctive faith, that men of simple modes of character are prone to antedate its consummation." Muir's "Canis" endnote, erased but partly legible, referred to the "dim simplicity of his character," with "none of the elfish sagacity of the hairy terriers."

————. *The Marble Faun, or the Romance of Monte Beni.* vol. 1. Boston: Houghton Mifflin, 1884. 2 pp. holographic index, mostly draft text. UOPWA.

The dog's latent intellect, a theme Muir developed in part from the theme of this novel, has been discussed in chapter three. His endnotes also rework earlier descriptions of the storm, interspersed with passages on oneness, animal equality and immortality.

————. *The Marble Faun, or The Romance of Monte Beni.* vol. 2. Boston: Houghton Mifflin, 1884. 1 p. holographic index, notes.

Muir's back page additions consist of only a few short notes, mostly revising earlier versions of the dog's "much mongrelized ancestors."

————. *Mosses from an Old Manse.* vol. 1. Boston: Houghton Mifflin, 1884. 4 pp. endnotes, index, draft text. UOPWA.

Hawthorne's appreciation for the human side of life Muir found appealing and suggestive of a broader unity of creation. He marked a noteworthy passage in "The Procession of Life," where the author appeals to an end of class or social distinctions: "the longer I reflect the less am I satisfied with the idea of forming a separate class of mankind on the basis of high intellectual power. At best it is but a higher development of innate gifts common to all." Later in the same essay Hawthorne reminded Muir of the great equalizer: the downtrodden should remember "that Death levels us all into one great brotherhood, and that another state of being will surely rectify the wrong of this."

Muir enlarged the thought and added an attack on crass commercialism. His endnote saw Stickeen as "a horizontal man child/ heart beating in accord with the universal beat of Nat[ure]/ Fellow-feeling develops with yrs. [of] brotherhood/ hopes fears joys griefs imagination memory soul as well as body a share of every celestial fire radiating from him to earth,- a share of immortality as surely as that wh cheers the best saint that ever walked on end/ quicken the natural current of outflowing sympathy & fellowship, back & forth between all god's creatures—so deplorably dammed up & dissipated in the swamps of business."

————. *Mosses from an Old Manse.* vol. II. Boston: Houghton Mifflin, 1884. 1 p. draft text, 1 index note; some text erased & illegible. UOPWA.

In "The New Adam and Eve," Hawthorne's comment on the power of imagination caught Muir's eye: "It is only through the medium of the imagination that we can lessen those iron fetters, which we call truth and reality, and make ourselves even partially sensible what prisoners we are." Muir was also taken by the New Englander's caveat on characterization in "The Old Apple Dealer." It seemed applicable to "Stickeen": "To confess the truth, it is not the easiest matter in the world to define and individualize a character like this which we are now handling. The portrait must be so generally negative that the most delicate pencil is likely to spoil it by introducing some too positive tint. Every touch must be kept down, or else you destroy the subdued tone which is absolutely essential to the whole effect."

On the back pages Muir drafted several notes on the dog he later erased, but one or two lines are still legible. The connection to Hawthorne's comments are clear, although Muir initialed the following aphorism to show its originality: "It is hard to know what prisoners we are (H) so far are we divorced from nature (JM)."

———. *Our Old Home, and English Note-Books*. vol. 1. Boston: Houghton Mifflin, 1884. 3 pp. holographic index, notes, draft text. UOPWA.

In addition to pursuing the theme of latency, as discussed in chapter three, Muir's endnotes show he was working on snippets of narrative describing the dog's first reaction to the crevasse, the transmigration theory, and the early incidents on the 1880 trip. He was "no coward," wrote Muir, willing to "plunge in waves breaking on the beach & swim like a seal."

———. *Our Old Home, and English Note-books*. vol. 3. Boston: Houghton Mifflin, 1884. 1 p. holographic index, notes, draft text. UOPWA.

In Hawthorne's English notebook of 1856, Muir highlighted this description of a striking dinner guest later identified as Macaulay: "There was a somewhat careless self-possession, large and broad enough to be called dignity; and the more I looked at him, the more I knew that he was a distinguished person." In the endnotes that statement was metamorphosed into another characterization of "Stickeen": "Canis good—careless (dull) self-possession broad enough & dull enough to be possibly dignity—but he kept his heart hidden as if the gloom of the great icy land had settled down about him."

————. *Our Old Home, and English Note-books.* vol. 4. Boston: Houghton Mifflin, 1884. 2 pp. holographic index, notes, draft text. UOPWA.

Amid several original aphorisms Muir's endnotes convert a comment by Hawthorne about the "bleak and blasty shore of the Irish Sea" into a somber, but disjointed, note on "Stickeen": "the winds are howling like wolves—as if the gray velvety gloom of his native land had settled down on him/ Bleak and blasty shore."

————. *The Scarlet Letter.* Boston: Houghton Mifflin, 1884. 3 pp. holographic draft text. UOPWA.

Muir took more direct ideas from "The Custom House," an autobiographical story preceding *The Scarlet Letter,* than from the novel proper. He particularly liked Hawthorne's comment on growth of the mind: "It contributes greatly towards a man's moral and intellectual health, to be brought into habits of companionship with individuals unlike himself, who care little for his pursuits, and whose sphere and abilities he must go out of himself to appreciate." He also noted a later comment in the same story on the drudgery of custom-house duties and the officer's dim future prospects: "A dreary look-forward this, for a man who felt it to be the best definition of happiness to live throughout the whole range of his faculties and sensibilities!"

In the lengthy endnotes, Muir developed his clock metaphor as discussed in chapter three, and, spinning off from Hawthorne's first comment quoted above, explored a series of ideas on Stickeen's initial "dullness": "Then the depths & shallows of his mind were revealed in full light & sympathy/ A hardy unchangeable evergreen—a crank; He seemed to have no mind, no feeling, only shallow glimmering instincts no soul no heart no ideas/ a sort of dull serenity of face lighted only by glances from his eyes that hinted something hidden & broke the darkness/ a dull silly semiimbecile look/ obstinate stubborn & tho so small was capable of heavy endurance." After an interlude of short pulses of words about the dog's character, Muir concludes his notes with the statement on unity and equality quoted in chapter three.

————. *Septimius Felton, with an Appendix containing The Ancestral Footstep.* Boston: Houghton Mifflin, 1884. 2 pp. holographic index, notes, draft text. UOPWA.

Most of Muir's notes are on other matters, but he tried some drafts on "Stickeen" here he later erased. Among them was a still-legible comment on instinct: "tis said that animals possess instincts that forewarns them of danger {not so Stick, afraid only when he looked into gulf & saw I meant to cross it}."

―――. *The Snow-Image and other Twice Told Tales*. Boston: Houghton, Mifflin, 1884. 2 pp. holographic index, notes, draft text. UOPWA.

Numerous pencil marks in the text indicate Muir's interest in Hawthorne's descriptions of nature, but no apparent correlation between these marks and Muir's short endnote: "(Canis) Never offered his head to be patted nor refused a caress, just didnt care Mild dull & respectable in deportment."

―――. *Twice-told Tales*. vol. 1. Boston: Houghton Mifflin, 1884. 2 pp. holographic index, notes, draft text. UOPWA.

Muir's endnotes seem to bear little relation to Hawthorne's narrative, but do provide more details about crossing the glacier: "In the long list of doggish oddities some of Stickines seemed new. Amid scenes so stern & so lovely I sat down on the brink & pondered well the way I had come seeing my demis[e] [illegible word] in imagination like a chart. I saw that I was recrossing at a higher level & was in a new unknow[n] section. It was getting late & the sky threatened. Would I return to the woods a mile or two distant make a fire & pass a hungry night & trust for a better day all of it before me or take this jump & trust to luck in not being called on to take it back. It was dangerous, but at times an influence beyond ones reasoning & control seems to lay hands on us & focus us on beyond our control / spellbound & doomed."

―――. *Twice-told Tales*. vol. 2. Boston: Houghton Mifflin, 1884. 2 pp. holographic endnotes, draft text, index. UOPWA.

"This son of the wilderness and pilgrim of the storm took his place silently in the midst of us," wrote Hawthorne in the story "The Seven Vagabonds." Muir's "little pilgrim of the storm" was Stickeen. In the endnotes Muir expands on the stormy day and its meaning. It "Made my sympathy for my animal relatives go farther & quickened them & made them surer," he wrote. It "Strengthened the chain of human sympathies & showed how far it reached beyond our own species." After a series of notes on Stickeen's doggy idiosyncracies he returned to the storm motif: "The roaring of the blast the roaring of a 1000 torrents were all massed into one roar & the mts rocks forests gls & the heavns were all one gray mass of gloom—but I had long been familiar with storm weather & knew that the stormier the greater the enjoyment as long as one keeps in right relation to it."

Herbert, George. *The Works of George Herbert in Prose and Verse*. Edited by Robert Aris Willmott. London: George Routledge & Sons, n.d. 3 pp. holographic topical index, notes, draft text. UOPWA.

That Muir loved poetry and knew its value is amply confirmed by his frequent margin marks in this book. No direct correlation is apparent between Herbert's work and Muir's endnotes, but the poet's impact is nevertheless clear in Muir's attempt to craft poetic descriptions of Stickeen, "A sad lit[tle] dumpling of a d[og]," whose "Soul & body bent & twisted in a howling whirlwind of fear." Later he tells the dog: "Ah my boy we've missed this time, we've lost the harmony of the thing—tanged in discard & caught n a trap."

Also in the endnotes is an outline of Muir's central message: "Here is a lit[tle] story that sheds light on d[og]s. We live apart/ we should sympathize."

Maclaren, Ian. *Beside the Bonnie Brier Bush*. New York: Dodd, Mead, 1895. 2 pp. holographic index, notes. UOPWA.

On page 317 of this book Muir found relevant to "Stickeen" the story of a horse named Jess, who refused to eat after the death of its master. "No man knows what a horse or a dog understands and feels," wrote Maclaren, "for God hath not given them our speech." Muir's endnote was a simple reference to the page and his code word "Canis."

Miller, Hugh. *The Life and Letters of Hugh Miller*. Peter Bayne. vol. 1. Boston: Gould & Lincoln, 1871. Inscribed inside front flyleaf: "To Mr. Muir, The Yosemite, California, with the kindest regards of I. Hall, New York, 1872." 4 pp. holographic index, notes, draft text. UOPWA.

Muir read and made notes in this first volume the same year he received it, then went back over it during the writing of "Stickeen." Most of his notes are strung together in tightly woven clusters like the following: "(Can) Frank outspoken effulgence of mirth/garrulous loquacious chatty."

They cover aspects of character he later expanded into long passages. One metaphor from Miller, describing friendship and solitude on a seashore working on the mind like waves on pebbles, Muir reworked for the dog story: "Stick[een] was a dif[ferent] dog after this day like a boulder after polishing in a torrent."

————. *The Life and Letters of Hugh Miller.* Peter Bayne. vol. 2. Boston: Gould & Lincoln, 1871. Inscribed: "To Mr. Muir with kindest regards of I. Hall." 3 pp. holographic index, notes, refs., quotes; margin marks throughout text. UOPWA.

Muir's metaphor of the clock, partly derived from this text, has been discussed in chapter three. Another passage Muir found of interest was a letter discussing "womans rights," as Muir noted in his endnote: "You are fretted, my own dear girl, by the bondage to frivolity, which sex and fashion impose upon you. No wonder you should, when one thinks of the sort of laws by which you are bound. The blockheads are a preponderating majority in both sexes; but somehow in ours the clever fellows contrive to take the lead and make the laws, whereas I suspect that in yours the more numerous party are tenacious of their privileges as such, and legislate both for themselves and the minority." Muir makes no further mention of the passage, so it is unclear what impact it might have had on his own thinking.

Montaigne, Michel Eyquem de. *The Essayes of Michael Lord of Montaigne.* Translated by John Florio. London: J. M. Dent, 1897. 5 v. Holographic notes in all volumes; numerous references to dogs marked throughout. HL.

It is clear from his endnotes that Muir found Montaigne a spiritual soul mate whose views on the equality of creation and on the intelligence of animals matched his own. In volume one, for example, Muir seconded Montaigne's notion of a created universe where man is one of many species. "And considering, that one selfe-same master (I meane that incomprehensible worlds-framer) hath placed all creatures in this his wondrous palace for his service, and that they, as well as we, are of his household: I say, it hath some reason to injoyne us, to shew some respect and affection towards them."

In chapters eleven and twelve of the second volume Muir marked nearly every page where the author, using anecdotal evidence, described characteristics of animals resembling humans. He especially liked the author's subtle attack on "Lord Man": "But when amongst the most moderate opinions, I meet with some discourses that goe about and labour to shew the neere resemblance betweene us and beasts, and what share they have in our greatest Priveleges, and with how much likelyhood they are compared unto us, truly I abate much of our presumption, and am easily removed from that imaginary soveraigntie that some give and ascribe unto us above all other creatures." The remarks about human ignorance of animal behavior seemed to Muir directly applicable to his own experience in 1880: "Whatsoever seemeth strange unto us, and we understand not, we blame and condemne. The likee beffaleth us in our judging of beasts. They have diverse qualities, which somewhat simbolize with ours: from which, we may comparatively draw some conjecture, but of such as are peculiar unto them, what know wee what they are?" Muir read Montaigne too late to be of much help on the "Stickeen" text—perhaps with the exception of the transmigration theory—but the reading nevertheless reinforced many of his own views on animals.

The *Oxford Book of English Verse, 1250-1900*. Edited by A. T. Quiller-Couch. Oxford: Clarendon Press, 1908. Inscribed to JM from Fairfield and Loulu Osborne, 20 Mar 1910. Extensive margin marks; notes and indexes cover front and back pages. UOPWA.

Muir never lost his love of poetry and read it whenever opportunity arose. Even verse he knew intimately from previous readings he returned to time and again for pleasure and inspiration. Knowing his passion for poetry, the Osborns gave him this anthology. In it was a sampling of Coleridge, including the *Rime of the Ancient Mariner,* which Muir reread with relish. The dog story was now in print, both in article and book form, but several couplets reminded him of his time on the Taylor glacier, and he marked them with his old code, "Stick": "And through the drifts the snowy clifts / Did send a dismal sheen:/ Nor shapes of men nor beasts we ken—/ The ice was all between./ . . . The ice did split with a thunderfit;/ The helmsman steer'd us through!"

Parkman, Francis. *A Half-century of Conflict.* 2 v. Boston: Little, Brown & Co., 1896 [c1892]. v. 1, $3/4$ pp. holographic notes; 2-line "Stickeen" note erased and illegible v. 2, $1/2$ p. page index and 1 "Stickeen" note. HL.

Muir's notes on dogs in volume one are not readable, but may have been connected to a line of text Muir marked: "He had a robust, practical brain, capable of broad views and large schemes." The language bears a resemblance to some of the later drafts of "Stickeen." Volume two has no apparent linkage between Parkman's text and Muir's brief endnote: "Canis sober solemn independent & disobedient/ Came out of every experience with obstinacy unimpaired."

————. *Count Frontenac and New France under Louis XIV.* Boston: Little, Brown & Co., 1896 [c1877]. 2 pp. holographic notes, draft "Stickeen" text (all erased), page index. HL.

The notes on dogs in the back of the volume cannot be fully reconstructed, but legible fragments indicate that Muir used the back pages to reiterate sentences about the dog's features and character. The last line hints at a relationship to Parkman's proclivity for Romantic rendering of frontier personalities: "no feature brought out to mark individuality or give anything picturesque."

————. *The Oregon Trail; Sketches of Prairie and Rocky-Mountain Life.* Boston: Little, Brown & Co., 1896 [c1872]. 2 $1/2$ pp. holographic notes; ca. $1/2$ page of draft "Stickeen" passages erased. HL.

The word fragments still legible make it apparent that Muir continued to work on characterization in the late stages of his "Stickeen's" preparation. His margin marks hint at the content and also demonstrate the textual relationship between Muir's story and Parkman's Romantic diction. For example, compare the language of the final draft of "Stickeen" with the following lines of text marked by Muir: (p. 182) "between him and me there was no other bond of sympathy than the slender and precarious one of a kindred race"; (pp. 257–8) "For the most part, a civilized white man can discover very few points of sympathy between his own nature and that of an Indian. With every disposition to do justice to their good qualities, he must be conscious that an impassable gulf lies between him and his red brethren."

————. *Pioneers of France in the New World.* Boston: Little, Brown & Co., 1896 [c1885]. 3 pp. holographic notes; passages on "Stickeen" partly erased. HL.

Muir continued the pattern observed above, working on the dog's qualities and trying out narrative combinations he—or possibly Helen after 1915—erased later. Parkman's description of Cartier's cautious approach to the cliffs before Quebec reminded Muir of his own glacial perils. "To most readers," he wrote, "it would seem the most likely thing in the O [world] to get caught in such networks of chasms & cracks, yet this is not so/ [By] careful exploration one may make a way in the most threatening difficulties & this in all my wanderings was the first time I had got caught. & even then only because I had taken one jump I could not take back/ Stick could have returned all his steps but the length of his intellect didnt reach backward that far."

Plutarch, *Plutarch's Lives*. John and William Langhorne, translators. Cincinnati: Applegate, 1856. Inside front cover: stenciled inscription: "D. Muir" 1 p. holographic index inside back pages; "Stickeen" passages inside front pages. UOPWA.

One of the few surviving volumes from the family library in Wisconsin, this book remained one of Muir's lifelong favorites. His notes demonstrates Muir's incessant search for references he could use to upgrade the language and improve the literary quality of the dog story. From Plutarch's story of Diogenes, Muir developed a metaphor comparing the independence of Stickeen to "Diogenes in his tub." By the final draft that comment had been replaced by another along the same line: "but Stickine seemed a very Diogenes, asking only to be let alone." Muir also used this book, as he had many others, to draft out short comments later worked into the dog story. One described Stickeen's exploratory prowess: "at the Ind villages we stopped at he could go through brier patches & thorny patches & the roughest rocks without scath, only on gls he hurt himself & once his little feet made stains at every step." The sentence made it to the final draft in a much revised and abbreviated form.

Renan, Ernest. *The Future of Science*. Boston: Roberts Bros., 1891. 1 p. holographic index (3 items), notes. UOPWA.

Muir found this French writer/philosopher's statement on the "grand ideal" worth noting: "There is a great central focus in which poetry, science, and morality are identical, in which to know, to admire, and to love are one and the same thing, in which all opposing sentiments drop away, in which human nature recognizes the high harmony of all its faculties and that grand act of adoration which sums up the tendency of its whole being towards the everlasting infinite, in the identity of its aim. The saint is he who devotes his life to this grand ideal and votes all the rest useless." But he was less impressed by the blanket condemnation of theology he found in the text. While he could agree that dogmatic theology was abhorrent, he rejected the author's conclusion that "of all studies most brutalizing, most destructive of all poetry, theology is the first." "Dont be too sure & complete," Muir responded, although his endnote did not elaborate.

Renan's comments on the "sympathetic reaction" of men to the graceful movements of a swan gave Muir pause to reflect on human-animal relationships: "I always believed in fair play, justice to animals. Never could draw the line /o/ [between] man & animals—less than ever after this adventure."

Romanes, George J. *Animal Intelligence.* New York: D. Appleton, 1883. Inside front page: Inscribed "John Muir, Martinez, California." Below is inscription: "To Wanda, nurse & friend & lover of all her feeble fellow mortals, on her fifteenth birthday, March 25th 1896. from her affectionate & admiring father." 3 pp. Muir holographic index, notes. UOPWA.

Muir's reading of Romanes, and its influence on his "Stickeen" manuscript, is discussed in chapter four. Among the notes already mentioned was the following, another spin-off from the Romanes text: "Can[us:] The attitude of man to the rest [of the] animal kingdom is unspeakably blind & mean/ His reasoning was not of a high order but it was as good as much purely human of a weak Know[ledge?] under similiar circumstances."

Ruskin, John. *Modern Painters.* vol. 1, part 1-2. New York: John Wiley & Sons, 1886. 2 pp. holographic index, selected quotes, lines of poetry, commentary & draft text. UOPWA.

This edition Muir acquired long after his first reading of Ruskin. It is part of a larger set, all of which show Muir's holographic markings, indicating he reread at least part of Ruskin's work even though he disliked some of the Englishman's opinions. In this volume Muir bracketed one of Ruskin's comments: "There are few things so great as death; and there is perhaps nothing which banishes all littleness of thought and feeling in an equal degree with its contemplation." The statement triggered a string of thoughts on dogs that Muir scribbled on the back pages: "Danger, sublimity/ too magnanimous to be moved with trifles—unteachable unresponsive dull immobility—wh in begger dogs might pass for dignity, cool moderate selfcontained unfamiliar as a philosopher or old cat."

————. *Modern Painters*. vol. 2, part 3, sections 1 & 2. New York: John Wiley & Sons, 1886. 2 pp. holographic index, commentary, aphorisms & draft text. UOPWA.

Without reference to the text, Muir's endnote incorporates an Addisonian metaphor he had noted in Taine's *History of English Literature*. It was dropped before the final draft of "Stickeen": "No cross {counter} influences to compensate the case/ He must cross that bridge of mirza or go back into the wild wood among wolves—poor babe in the wood, bounded by the sea and gl[acier]s desert & he knew what his fate would be/ had heard the wolves howl many a night."

————. *The Stones of Venice*. vol. 2. New York: John Wiley & Sons, 1886. 2 pp. holographic index, notes, draft text. UOPWA.

Another example of Muir's eclecticism. In this case he perceives Stickeen's character through a Ruskin discussion on the nature of the Gothic mind. The Englishman, attributing architectural style in northern England to the influences of weather, said on page 205 that Northern Gothic suggests "Strength of will, independence of character, resoluteness of purpose, impatience of undue control, and that general tendency to set the individual reason against authority, and the individual deed against destiny." Muir marked the passage, and in his footnotes wrote simply: "205 Canis."

————. *Time and Tide, By Weare and Tyne: Twenty-five Letters to a Working Man of Sunderland on the Laws of Work*. New York: John Wiley & Sons, 1886. 3 pp. holographic index, notes, draft text. UOPWA.

This volume contains Ruskin's ninth lecture on "The Eagle's Nest," which brought a sharp response from Muir because of its rejection of natural selection. Muir liked other Ruskinian passages, especially a flowing statement that gave Muir some ideas about Alaska and the dog: "(A[laska] Ex[cellent]) . . . / transition from irrational dullness to irrational excitement/ . . . The Kingdom of the Sky (A Ex/ (154 Serenely minded dog Ex) undoggish/ uncharitable nature/ Virtue & faithfulness ignoble creature/ simple-minded dullish."

Scott, Sir Walter. *The Abbott*. In *Waverley Novels*. v. 1. New York: George Routledge & Sons [1876?]. 3 pp. holographic notes, draft text. HL.

Muir wrote narrative fragments of his adventure in all the volumes of this Waverley edition. In many cases the notes have no direct ties to Scott's text, as if Muir were simply using the back pages for scratch paper.

This appears to be the case with *The Abbott*. Muir's notes show three separate reading sequences, with "Stickeen" notes following the last page reference. Culling through them turns up few new details but provides a broad if desultory overview of Muir's state of mind as well as his writing method. Stickeen, he asked, "What is he good for[?] nothing that I know of said the minister but pity." Yet "No fish seemd more at home in water than he nor bird in air as he cleared crevasses"—a point Muir's editor wanted to bury to enhance the plot.

————. *Anne of Geierstein*. In *Waverley Novels*. v. 2. New York: George Routledge & Sons, [1876?]. 3 pp. holographic endnotes. HL.

In this volume Muir's endnotes correlate in several instances with Scott's text. In chapter fifteen, for example, Scott describes the effect of Anne's touch on the tormented prisoner Arthur Philipson: "Courage was restored to his heart, vigour and animation to his benumbed and bruised limbs; such influence does the human mind, when excited to energy, possess over the infirmities of the human body." Muir's endnote, referring to "Stickeen," claimed that "The influence seems well nigh miraculous that the mind possesses over the body in perils such as these strength without food & courage & nerve of steel on the edge of death."

In chapter two, Scott describes a conversation in which the Swiss maiden tries to build courage in Arthur to attempt a dangerous feat of mountaineering. "But instead of being a step to be taken on the level and firm earth," writes the narrator, "it was one which must cross a dark abyss, at the bottom of which a torrent surged and boiled with incredible fury." The sentence provided a literary backdrop for Muir's long efforts to draft the crucial line on Stickeen's first sign of intelligence. In the back pages he wrote: "As I kneeled on the brink of the gulf & surveyed the curved wedge of ice & its dangerous attachment at either end Stickeen came beside me his head close to mine looked into the abyss & then into my face with intelligent concern as if saying Surely you dont mean to try to cross here. Intelligent appreciation of the danger This was the first evidence of sympathy between us Comprehending evidently the difficulty in expressions of countenance." Despite a dozen or more different versions of this singular incident he drafted in other books and later in notebooks and loose pages, his final draft is a close cousin to the version recorded here.

————. *The Antiquary*. In *Waverley Novels*. v. 3. New York: George Routledge & Sons, [1876?]. 3 pp. holographic notes. HL.

Muir reminisced about boyhood in these notes, developing some ideas that later appear in *Boyhood and Youth*. The notes on "Stickeen" are fragmentary and bear little relation to Scott's narrative. "all animals assist & defend each other in times of deadly peril," he wrote, adding that "Man is a good climber, dogs not . . . Poor forlorn heart."

————. *Betrothed*. In *Waverley Novels*. v. 4. New York: George Routledge & Sons, [1876?]. 3 pp. holographic notes. HL.

A sequence of fragmented notes, not connected to Scott's story, describes the dog's looks and manners. Muir ends this sequence with another version of oneness: "Now in excess of joy at his deliverance from such desperate danger he became the bravest d[og] of dogkind/ & never have I in all my studies of & communings with animals has my opinion & feeling that we are direct relatives [of] fellow mortals bone of our bone & flesh of our flesh been more confirmed & corroborated than on that danger[ous] day on the Alask gl with Stickine."

————. *The Black Dwarf; Montroise; Lammermoor*. In *Waverley Novels*. v. 5. New York: George Routledge & Sons, [1876?]. 4 pp. holographic notes. HL.

A lengthy series of notes, but only a few on "Stickeen." Scott's "A Legend of Montrose" claimed "distinctions of rank are readily set aside among those who are made to be sharers of common danger. Muir's endnote extends that idea: "As the distinctions of rank are naturally set aside in presence of danger so also are those of species & of course Stickine & I were friends in distress & equal."

————. *Count Robert of Paris*. In *Waverley Novels*. v. 6. New York: George Routledge & Sons, [1876?]. 2 pp. holographic notes. HL.

Muir's notes, showing only faint traces of Scott's diction but close parallels to his style, consist of a long and mostly redundant iteration of previously recorded statements on Stickeen's confrontation of the abyss, his intelligence, and oneness with animals. One example will suffice: Stickeen's life before the adventure, wrote Muir, "went slowly quietly on unbroken by excitement like a stream in a level bog."

————. *Fair Maid of Perth*. In *Waverley Novels*. v. 7. New York: George Routledge & Sons, [1876?]. 3 pp. holographic notes. HL.

Chapter three has already provided one example of Muir's debt to *Fair Maid*. The rest of his notes follow patterns of development, phraseology, and content similar to those in other novels of this series.

————. *The Fortunes of Nigel*. In *Waverley Novels*. v. 8. New York: George Routledge & Sons, [1876?]. 3 pp. holographic notes. HL.

Taking a cue from Scott's description of the contrast between the homely physical features and the favorable personality of Jenkin Vincent, Muir drew a word picture of Stickeen, who "Seemed determined that come what may he would never deliver his comic dignity to be degraded by undue familiarity/ had to judge character by external forms." Other notes repeat and reformulate previous descriptions of character.

————. *Guy Mannering*. In *Waverley Novels*. v. 9. New York: George Routledge & Sons, [1876?]. 1 $1/4$ pp. holographic notes. HL.

Scott's line in chapter twenty-one announcing the hero's intent "to make a further excursion through this country while this fine frosty weather serves," reminded Muir of his Alaskan adventure, as his endnotes indicate. He also tried a tentative closing line: "So ended the great & dreadful ice-day to doggie & I."

————. *The Heart of Mid-Lothian*. In *Waverley Novels*. v. 10. New York: George Routledge & Sons, [1876?]. 4 pp. holographic notes. HL.

The notes on "Stickeen" here are extensive and come before Muir's page indexing. This pattern, seen in other Scott novels, indicates that Muir used the blank pages to record notes before reading the text. Most of these notes describe ideas and points of character already discussed, although one passage is a reminiscence about the early Wisconsin years that does not again appear until the publication of *Boyhood and Youth*. "I always loved dogs & many a time they have brought tears to my eyes/ Scotch colley, when I left home knew me when my neighbors didnt in changed dress & seemed in agony of joy groaned & screamed one eager sniff of my feet/ Carlo. (could not take dog with me but first summer a man loaned me St Bernard because he would be more comfortable in cool mtns the home of his ancestors/ He believed all animals fellow mortals."

From Scott, Muir probably adapted a line never used in the final draft: "If he had any fun or affection then like an old fashioned Lowland Scotchman he took great care to conceal it."

———. *Ivanhoe*. In *Waverley Novels*. v. 11. New York: George Routledge & Sons, [1876?]. 3 pp. holographic notes; index. HL.

The extensive notes on the back pages follow a familiar pattern of wandering into free-form characterizations disconnected to the text he was reading, but there are some exceptions. For example, Muir found useful Scott's observation on the psychology of stress: "A moment of peril," said Scott, "is often also a moment of open-hearted kindness and affection. We are thrown off our guard by the general agitation of our feelings, and betray the intensity of those, which, at more tranquil periods, our prudence at least conceals, if it cannot altogether suppress them." Muir condensed that into a poignant sentence that did not surface in later drafts: "Moments of peril lay us bare & make us known to ourselves as well as to our companions."

———. *Kenilworth*. In *Waverley Novels*. v. 12. New York: George Routledge & Sons, [1876?]. 1 p. holographic notes, page index, draft text. HL.

"Onward with Firm unvacillating steps & bounds," wrote Muir in an imaginary conversation with the dog, with "nerve to walk a narrow plank across so terrible a gulf."

———. *Old Mortality*. In *Waverley Novels*. v. 13. New York: George Routledge & Sons, [1876?]. 1 $1/4$ pp. holographic notes; index, draft text. HL.

In this fanciful tale, where the hero is almost overcome by the raw forces of nature, Muir found a model for expressing his own predicament at the crevasse. His endnotes, preceded by the code "Stick," refer to page numbers where he highlighted relevant text. In chapter thirty-nine, for instance, Muir marked Scott's probing of the Henry Morton's state of mind when confronting the danger before him: "The instinct of self-preservation seldom fails, even in the most desperate circumstances, to recall the human mind to some degree of equipoise, unless when altogether distracted by terror, and Morton was obliged to the danger in which he was placed for complete recovery of his self-possession." The confrontation described in chapter forty-three was so close to Muir's own experience he gave it special emphasis in his endnote reference. Morton approaches a "doubtful and terrific bridge" that was "wet and slippery" and "sixty feet from the bottom." He "resolved to attempt the passage, and, fixing his eye firm on a stationary object on the other side, without allowing his head to become giddy, or his attention to be distracted by the flash, the foam, and the roar of the waters around him, he strode steadily and safely along the uncertain bridge."

————. *Peveril of the Peak*. In *Waverley Novels*. v. 14. New York: George Routledge & Sons, [1876?]. 4 pp. holographic notes, draft text. HL.

A lengthy series of fragmented notes on "Stickeen," some showing connections to word patterns in the novel but most reiterating other material on the dog story. A few of the more interesting examples: "A slow grim dogged determination to do as he liked. . . . One would suppose he carried in his trust some heavy solemn care or he was stupid. . . . You have the courage of ignorance you little dolt you dont know danger when you see it."

Scott's quotation from the opening lines of an unidentified play, where Oswald replies to Acasto's question "Can she not Speak?", influenced Muir's thinking on the dog's mute language: "If speech be only in accented sounds,/ Framed by the tongue and lips, the maiden's dumb;/ But if by quick and apprehensive look,/ By motion, sing, and glance, to give each meaning/ Express as clothed in language, be term'd speech,/ She hath that wondrous faculty; for her eyes,/ Like the bright stars of heaven, can hold discourse,/ Though it be mute and soundless." In the endnotes Muir jotted down "quick apprehensive look by motion sign & glance to you each meaning," a phrasing that gradually evolved into the "speaking look" Stickeen gave him in the final draft of 1897.

————. *The Pirate*. In *Waverley Novels*. v. 15. New York: George Routledge & Sons, [1876?]. 2 pp. holographic notes, page index, draft text. HL.

Muir referred to this novel repeatedly during the preparation of "Stickeen," as his endnotes indicate. A passage on fortune-tellers gave him ideas about expressing the innocent beginning on the day of the adventure: "not the faintest shadow of our coming trial fortold," he wrote. A text reference to the unusual silence of "very aquatic birds" that "forebore their usual flight and screams," led Muir to write about the avian impact of the storm that surrounded him and the dog: "All the gulls were driven from the sea & the largest birds from the sky/ not a wing to be seen the moving storm took all the sky to itself." On page 412 of the text, Scott's summary of the heroine's life, claiming that "from all who approached her" she enjoyed "an affection enhanced by reverence," provided Muir with another way to verbalize his feelings. His endnote simply said: "412 Stick *v.g.* Affection enhanced by reverence."

Among these endnotes Muir wrote an isolated phrase that he had read before in the poetry of Robert Burns: "Wee sleeket cowern timorous beastie." In a later draft of the "Stickeen" text Muir identified Burns by name and tried to incorporate other short quotations,[3] but the final draft omitted all but the "beastie" phrase, slightly modified.

————. *Quentin Durward*. In *Waverley Novels*. v. 16. New York: George Routledge & Sons, [1876?]. 3 pp. holographic notes; draft text; page index. HL.

A horse in this novel exhibits characteristics Muir relates to "Stickeen." A dying man's last request was to care for Klepper his old companion: "He will never fail you at need," he said, "—night and day, rough and smooth, fair and foul, warm stables and the winter sky, are the same to Klepper." Muir's endnote repeated the statement, with one addition: "warm stables & the wintry sky are the same to Klepper [and] Stickine."

Elsewhere Muir found a "*v.g.*" statement relevant to the dog. The countess replies to a question from Isabella: "necessity, my friend, is the mother of courage, as of invention." A reference to being "hanged by morn" spurred Muir to compare natural and civilized forms of demise: "Never had contempt of death tho would regard my fate in the heart of a gl as clear & noble/ compared to that of a mean accident or death in a bed or street. Life & death hunked in a single glint of the hatchet."

Not connected to the novel was an endnote anecdote about Stickeen's antics prior to the experience on the Taylor glacier. "In the gulf of ebon darkness," wrote Muir, "walled in by the forest we saw a portentous wedge of light in the water that seemed to be made by some leviathan of the deep. clearing his impetuous way Never it came when in the bulge of light in front the little black head of Stickine was revealed." After many expansions and revisions, Muir incorporated it into the final draft of 1897. Johnson excised it before publishing the article, but Muir restored it in the text of 1909.

————. *Redgauntlet*. In *Waverley Novels*. v. 17. New York: George Routledge & Sons, [1876?]. 4 pp. holographic notes, draft text. HL.

Numerous dog anecdotes in this novel are referenced in Muir's lengthy endnotes, which are interspersed with disjointed thoughts about Stickeen. Sentence fragments are strung together like colorful beads looking for a necklace. One example: "annoying idiosincrasies, steadiness & indiffrence of temper nearly like apathy/ heavy dignity of stupid indifference/ povertie of spirit, absurd caprice of hiding till boat left/ stormy smiles of the moon thro the racing clds/ Long wedge of light of portentious dimensions."

————. *Rob Roy*. In *Waverley Novels*. v. 18. New York: George Routledge & Sons, [1876?]. 2 pp. holographic notes, draft text. HL.

Muir had less to say about "Stickeen" on the back pages of this book than in most of the other Waverley novels, but nevertheless he managed to draft a few lines, most of them triggered by Scott's remark that he "never heard entreaties for life poured forth with such agony of spirit." Wrote Muir: "ineffable terror/ecstasy of fear (Stickine)/ . . . such eloquence of agony/ . . . a depth & hollow volume to the sound of his agonizing cries so unlike the tones of so small a dog/ but never before did the distance /0/ dog & man seem so narrow/."

————. *St. Ronan's Well*. In *Waverley Novels*. v. 19. New York: George Routledge & Sons, [1876?]. 3 pp. holographic page index, notes, draft text. HL.

After reading Scott's description of the facial features of a squire, Muir jotted a short note about Stickeen's "cunning *eye-gleams*." Most of his notes follow a familiar pattern of stringing words together in alliterative phrases that might be used later. One such string: "Intimacy vehemence of tone/ Invincible composure of manner/ a pitiful helpless microcosm of misery/ irrefragable grounds of action."

————. *The Talisman*. In *Waverley Novels*. v. 20. New York: George Routledge & Sons, [1876?]. 4 pp. holographic notes; page index, draft text. HL.

References to dogs appear frequently in Scott's novels, and Muir's notes show that he read all these passages with an eye for words and phrases possibly of use in drafting his own dog story. The endnotes in this novel contain the most extensive set of references to "Stickeen" of all Scott's works in Muir's library. Most of them bear only faint relation to the text, as if Muir used Scott as a launching pad for an independent journey of exploration, rather than as a narrow pathway through a forbidding jungle. In some cases these endnotes are new descriptive ventures, in others they replicate older versions of the evolving narrative. Scattered among short strings of words are longer passages that elucidate the storm's fury, the dog's character, or the glacier's features. Some of the more innovative examples: on the "gashed & wrinkled bosum of the gl[acier]" were "rills & streams enough to gladden a 1000 msq [mosquitoes]"; "The gashed wilderness of ice & the gloomy crawling clds rendered the sounds of the threatening winds fearfully solemn/ the sun shot thro the clds irradiating their edges & changing from dazzling splendor to dull boding gloom."

One anecdote from childhood he told here but never repeated: "When a boy my father bot me a Ind[ian?] frog & I determined to teach him to jump [illeg] & string wh resulted in being pitched over his head I dont know how many times. Once urged to jump a muddy creek he came down rock heavy in the middle of it lack of intelligence[.] How dif Stickine."

————. *Waverley*. In *Waverley Novels*. v. 21. New York: George Routledge & Sons, [1876?]. 2 pp. holographic notes, page index; no draft text. HL.

Two Muir references accent this otherwise prosaic collection of notes not related to "Stickeen." Both use Muir's "Stick" code, with "g[ood]" added. The first is to a line in the text, highlighted by a holographic margin line and the word "Stik," which at first glance bears no conceivable relation to the manuscript. It reads: "The wild revelry of the feast, for Mac-Ivor kept open table for his clan, served in some degree to *stun* reflection." What Muir made of this sentence is uncertain. Perhaps he saw it as analogous to the storm's impact on his own mood as he and Stickeen struck out to cross the glacier. The pencil marks he made do not match the light hand observed in the notations made in other books by Scott. They are reminiscent of his labored scrawl of later years, suggesting that he went back over this volume during the 1908 effort to draft the book manuscript.

The second reference is more obvious; it refers to a passage describing Waverley's happy mood on the night before the "approaching dangers of the morrow."

————. *Woodstock*. In *Waverley Novels*. v. 22. New York: George Routledge & Sons, [1876?]. 4 pp. holographic notes, page index, draft text. HL.

The last volume in the Scott series, but not the least to Muir. He marked a passage that brought back more memories of the dog: "there was something about the Independent so dark and mysterious, so grim and grave, that the more open spirit of the keeper felt oppressed, and, if not over-awed, at least kept in doubt concerning him." Muir's endnote said the dog must "have taken pains & practiced some sort of self-denial to ensure such steady unpunctuality. . . . So pensive deeply wrapped in his own business could spend no time on me. . . . never in any way disciplined he did as he liked/ mettlesome."

Extending this portrayal, Muir added some humorous detail that does not appear elsewhere: Stickeen, he reported, "went to the Presbyterian church on the Fort Wrangel Trail every Sunday accompanied by curs of every mixture from wolves pure & simple to lordly newfoundlands used to haul supplies up the Stickine River on the ice to the Cassiar gold mines." There he "behaved as well as any of the congregation white or Indian [dogs] & returned as much edified perhaps as most other most decent of Wrangel dogs."

Shelley, Percy Bysshe. *The Poetical Works of Percy Bysshe Shelley*. Edited by Mrs. Shelley. v. 1. Boston: Houghton, Osgood & Co., 1880 [c1855]. 2 pp. holographic notes, page index, draft text. HL.

Muir found in "The Revolt of Islam" a line he could relate to Stickeen: "I have heard," said the poet, "friendly sounds from many a tongue/ Which was not human—the lone nightingale/ Has answered me with her most soothing song,/ Out of her ivy bower, when I sat pale/ With grief, and sighed beneath; from many a dale/ The antelopes who flocked for food have spoken/ With happy sounds, and motions, that avail/ Like man's own speech; and such was not the token/ Of waning night, whose calm by that proud neigh was broken." In an endnote Muir wrote a much abbreviated and slightly modified version: "Can[us]) I have heard friendly sounds from many a tongue wh was not human/ All things a common nature."

———. *The Poetical Works of Percy Bysshe Shelley*. Edited by Mrs. Shelley. v. 2. Boston: Houghton, Osgood & Co., 1880 [c1855]. 2 pp. holographic notes; draft text. HL.

Almost every line in volume two of this collection had meaning for Muir. Many passages he related to his own manuscript. In "Hymn to Mercury," a Shelley couplet, Muir transformed "Not swifter a swift thought

of woe or weal/ Darts through the tumult of a human breast" into a plain-
tive comment: "Can[is]) . . . tumult of a human breast/ Lay down & raved
in dispair/ Confronted with death in the barest desolation." From "Julian
and Maddalo" Muir bracketed a stanza that seemed especially pertinent:
"A lovelier toy sweet Nature never made;/ A serious, subtle, wild, yet gentle
being,/ Graceful without design, and unforeseeing;/ With eyes—O! speak
not of her eyes! which seem/ Twin mirrors of Italian heaven, yet gleam/
With such deep meaning as we never see/ But in the human countenance."
Muir condensed this passage in an endnote: "(Can) every meaning in his
face ever seen in a human countenance, quick delicate trembling sensibility to anger when it came."

    "The Witch of Atlas" influenced Muir's portrayal of the Taylor Bay
glacier: "This lady never slept," wrote Shelley, "but lay in trance/ All night
within the fountain—as in sleep./ Its emerald crags glowed in her beauty's
glance;/ Through the green splendour of the water deep/ She saw the con-
stellations reel and dance/ Like fire-flies—and withal did ever keep/ The
tenour of her contemplations calm,/ With open eyes, closed feet, and folded
palm." Muir's endnote interpretation: "Sinius nerves string again in sleep/
. . . Light on gl. Emerald cliffs & crags, myriads of irised needles infinitely
firm & keen clustered on the crystal forests a thousand times more numerous than lvs of green on a gl mead[ow]."

Smollett, Tobias George. *The Adventures of Peregrine Pickle.* 2 vols. London:
    George Routledge & Sons, 1890. v. 1: 1 page index note; 3 notes; 1 draft
    text line. v. 2: 1 p. holographic draft text; no page index notes. HL.

    Smollett's prose gave Muir a few ideas he scratched out on the back
pages. He marked a line in volume one where Pickle's "sudden transition
from fear to joy occasioned a violent agitation both in his mind and body."
In volume two Muir moved away from Smollett's text to jot down a few
scattered thoughts about the dog. "Never was soul disguised in plainer
unspeaking features," he wrote. "I began to observe him with curiosity
when so many oddities came from so smooth & dull cobblestone of an
animal/ Stick was strictly glacial to every advance I made scratching his
ears calling him good & clapping his smooth cobblestone flanks he always
showed an aspect of ice/ His face seemed to be without muscles/ it was
always in all weathers the same/ Stoical indifference to what would make
others dance & sparkle & bark & bristle/ swelled up his voice into massive volumes wonderful from so small a source."

Taine, Hippolyte A. *History of English Literature*. Abridged from the translation of H. Van Laun, and edited by John Fiske. New York: Henry Holt, 1876. 7 pp. holographic index, notes, draft text. UOPWA.

When Muir acquired this well-used library book is not known, but he made extensive use of the outer wrappings to draft "Stickeen" notes. They demonstrate that Muir owed a profound debt to Taine for opening his eyes to classical literature he had either ignored or not known before. Through Taine, for instance, he first became acquainted with the writings of Thomas Browne, as his endnote proves: "[Page] 101 Sir Thomas Browne Especially the "urnburial" in Bohns library—get this book or all 4 vols." As we have seen, he read Browne thoroughly in late 1896 or early 1897, and made some last-minute revisions to the dog manuscript based on his reading.

In Taine Muir also read Addison's "Vision of Mirza," an allegorical verse on human morality. Initially Muir worked the title into a line of the "Stickeen" text, but later abandoned it. See also the comments under Ruskin's *Modern Painters*, vol. 2. Taine's quote from Dryden gave Muir some useful imagery to use in describing the dog's mental state: "Dryden/ As cold & unemotional as a small level gl[acier] curled up on a blue shadow. The only keen thing his eyes."

The sources of other draft passages of "Stickeen" are less clear, but a painstaking analysis of the extensive notes in this volume should prove rewarding. Many notes found here were later repeated or revised in the back pages of other volumes, indicating that Muir projected his ideas in a cycle that slowly upgraded and converted raw notes into sentences and paragraphs he could later pick from to construct a manuscript.

Thoreau, Henry D. *A Week on the Concord and Merrimack Rivers*. Boston: Ticknor & Fields, 1849. New and revised edition, 1868. 4 pp. holographic index, notes, draft text on end pages; extensive marginalia throughout. UOPWA.

Muir reread and indexed this and the following volume of Thoreau while working on "Stickeen," and took a few notes of possible use to him later. This text has extensive holographic markings throughout, though it cannot be determined when they were made. In his endnotes, Muir later added code words to identify texts he thought applicable to projects of current interest. Most of these codes relate to his book on Alaska, but some indicate his obsession with "Stickeen." One passage from Thoreau on heroes (p. 401) Muir thought had a direct bearing on the dog: "There have been heroes from whom this world seemed expressly prepared, as if creation had at last succeeded; whose daily life was the stuff of which our dreams are made, and whose presence enhanced the beauty and ampleness of Nature herself." Muir's endnote says simply: "Stick enhanced the bounty & abundance of Nat," adding "JM" to give it his own cachet.

Thoreau, Henry D. *Walden*. Boston: Ticknor & Fields, 1862. 2 pp. holographic index on end pages. UOPWA.

    While he worked on "Stickeen" Muir found *Walden* less useful than *A Week on the Concord and Merrimack Rivers*. Scanning his earlier notes he noted one passage in *Walden* that seemed relevant, in which Thoreau describes working his beanfield while listening to the birds: "When I paused to lean on my hoe, these sounds and sights I heard and saw any where in the row, a part of the inexhaustible entertainment which the country offers." Muir marked the passage and recorded in the endnote: "Calm & sympathy of nat[ure]/ Can) Heroic unmixed joy."

Tyndall, John. *Hours of Exercise in the Alps*. New York: D. Appleton, 1871. 4 pp. holographic topical index, notes, comments, draft text. UOPWA.

    This was another book Muir acquired long before the 1890s, and to which he returned while drafting his manuscript. He used it to develop ideas for describing Alaskan glaciers. In the midst of his notes, he inserted a thought on "Stickeen": "(Ex[cellent] Canis) his little heart squeezed by dreadful anxiety/ A little cld of anxiety began to settle about me wh speedily grew thick & heavy."

# Endnotes

1. Thomas Cowles noted that Herbert Spencer's *Social Statics* (185) only implied this linkage that Bagehot made explicit. Bagehot's first published essays on the subject preceded publication of *Origin of the Species*. See "Malthus, Darwin and Bagehot: a Study in the Tranference of a Concept," *Isis* 26 (December 1936): 341–48.
2. Frederick Turner, *Rediscovering America: John Muir in His Time and Ours* (New York: Viking Penguin, 1985), 74.

3.  See page 80 of the *Stickeen* blue notebook, *The John Muir Papers, 1858–1957*. Microform Edition. Ronald H. Limbaugh and Kirsten Lewis, eds. (Alexandria, VA: Chadwyck-Healey, Inc., 1986), 33/01370.

# Index

Ronald H. Limbaugh is a native of Idaho where he earned his M.A. in 1962 and his Ph.D. in 1967, both in history from the University of Idaho. He has written and published numerous books and articles on various aspects of American history with an emphasis on the West and the writings of John Muir. Director of the John Muir Center for Regional Studies at the University of the Pacific in Stockton, California, Limbaugh also occupies the Rockwell Hunt Chair of California History and teaches a variety of courses. In addition, he is an active member of several professional historical organizations and serves as executive director of the Conference of California Historical Societies.